DATE DUE

APR 2 0 1971			
SEP 2 3 1974			

BRO
DART Printed in U.S.A.

W/D

COLLINS

Oxford University Press
London Edinburgh Glasgow Leipzig Copenhagen
New York Toronto Melbourne Capetown
Bombay Calcutta Madras Shanghai
Humphrey Milford Publisher to the UNIVERSITY

COLLINS

BY

H. W. GARROD

Fellow of Merton College
Professor of Poetry in the
University of Oxford

THE FOLCROFT PRESS, INC.

First Published 1928

Reprinted 1969

CONTENTS

PREFACE

THE pages that follow are something between an essay and a commentary; and if any one either objects to the method of criticism or thinks that I might better have employed my leisure than by examining with this degree of minuteness a poet who is certainly not among the great poets of the world, I do not know that I have any completely satisfactory answer. For my method: I may perhaps plead that, if it belongs to some other century than that in which I have the good luck to live, it is not necessarily on that account out of date. As for my author: I was not wholly free, but was directed to him by an accident which the opening paragraphs of my essay sufficiently explain. Forty years ago a distinguished critic, who is still with us,[1] was bold to affirm that the power to appreciate Collins was 'an almost infallible test of a man's taste for the highest forms of poetic art'. I accept that; but perhaps in a sense somewhat different from what was intended.

[1] I had hardly written this when it ceased to be true. The reference is to Sir Edmund Gosse, by whose death the study of eighteenth-century literature loses one of its most attractive advocates.

I think it likely that there is no better education in poetry than can be won by distinguishing between the true and the false in Collins. In the Odes of 1746 Mr. Swinburne found 'hardly a single false note': 'and not many', he adds, 'less than sweet or strong'. With the second part of that criticism I agree cordially; but the first part of it I think as untrue as it could well be. Some of my commentary will seem, accordingly, ungracious and fault-finding. I had no wish to make it that; and if here and there I have not kept a just control of my emphasis, I hope that that will be put down to want of art in me, and not to a lack of goodwill. I deprecate the exaggerated praise of Collins for the reason that it makes him less interesting than he is. Where the greatest poetry is in question, I cannot count him to have attained. Yet it is just on this account that I think the study of him, even the minute study of him, well worth while. His failure is at once more interesting, and less damaging to him, than the ascription of success. But it is difficult to mark this failure without seeming to hunt faults. Nor is the task made easier by the circumstance that of Collins himself we know so little. It is a thousand pities that we do not know more of him than we do. But the tragedy of his poetry

Preface 9

is well pointed by his friend Thomson—if indeed
it is of Collins that Thomson wrote:

> For oft the heavenly fire, that lay concealed
> Amongst the sleeping embers, mounted fast,
> And all its native light anew revealed.
> Oft as he traversed the cerulean field,
> And marked the clouds that drove before the
>   wind,
> Ten thousand glorious systems would he build,
> Ten thousand great ideas filled his mind;
> But with the clouds they fled, and left no trace
>   behind.

Not no trace. But a line of light something between a pillar of fire and a pillar of cloud.

Thomson's lines might have been written of
Coleridge; and again and again, writing about
Collins, I have been reminded of Coleridge. In
the defect of our material, it is not possible to do
more than hint the parallel. But I have the suspicion that the lines of likeness run deep.

H. W. G.

COLLINS AND THE WARTONS

IN the early part of 1928 I was honoured by an invitation from the Council of the British Academy to deliver the annual Warton Lecture. The Lecture commemorates Thomas Warton the younger, who was Professor of Poetry in Oxford from 1757 to 1767, and whose *History of English Poetry* embodies, with defects of learning incidental to the time, qualities sometimes absent from learned work—freshness and warmth, a free sense of the pleasure that there is in poetry, and an instinct for communicating that pleasure. The year 1928 marked, I was reminded, the bicentenary of Warton's birth; and it was natural that I should cast round for a subject which should be near to Warton, which should illustrate tendencies in taste and criticism that he either forwarded or followed. Of Warton himself the praise had been sufficiently spoken in 1910, by the first Warton Lecturer; by a scholar [1] whose wide and catholic taste, as well as the direction of some of his special interests in poetry, gave him considerable likeness

[1] W. P. Ker.

to Warton. But I conceived that I should have
Warton in sufficient remembrance if, in a year
especially belonging to him, I took for my subject
a poet with whom he was connected, not only by
the tie of familiar friendship, but by common
studies in poetry and by a common conception of
the nature of poetry. It was to be near Warton
that Collins came to Oxford in 1754. That was
five years before his death. But already then his
mortal sickness was upon him. He was not able
without assistance to drag himself from his lodging
in St. Aldate's to Warton's rooms in Trinity. In
what tragedy the visit ended I have reason to be
reminded daily; for my windows in Oxford look
directly down on the spot where Gilbert White of
Selborne speaks of seeing him 'in a very affecting
situation, struggling and conveyed by force, in
the arms of two or three men, towards the parish
of St. Clement's, where there was a house which
took in such unhappy objects'. When at a later
date Collins was removed to Chichester, both
Tom Warton and his brother Joseph were among
the friends—it is to be feared, few in number
—whose occasional visits cheered his last se-
clusion.

Perhaps neither of them thought him a great
poet. Thomas Warton, it is true, in the second

volume[1] of his *History of English Poetry*, speaks, in
a footnote, of 'my lamented friend Mr. William
Collins, whose Odes will be remembered while
any taste for true poetry remains'. But that was
in 1778; and by that date Collins' Collected
Works had gone through three editions.[2] Thrice,
again, in his third volume Warton goes out of his
way to mention 'the late Mr. Collins of Chichester'—not, however, as a poet, but as a student of
Elizabethan literature. Joseph Warton, in a footnote to one of the later editions of his Essay on
Pope, speaks of 'the strong and fruitful imagination' of Collins; yet seems to rank him, even so,
a little below West and Mason and Akenside.
Yet if neither of them esteemed him a great poet,
both of them, I think, had a good deal to do with
making him a poet.

The more powerful influence was, it may be
surmised, that of Joseph. Of the two brothers,
Tom Warton was certainly the better scholar,
very likely the better poet—he had greater leisure
and opportunity to be both. Yet often I seem to
myself to detect in Joseph Warton the note of

[1] Section xxxiii, p. 508, 1840.
[2] I reckon as the first edition of the Collected Works, not
Langhorne's, but the eleventh volume of Fawkes and Woty's
Poetical Calendar (1763): the twelfth volume adds the Ode
on the Death of Thomson.

a more original mind—a judgement from which
Tom Warton, I fancy, would not have dissented.
I do not know that Tom Warton ever wrote better
poetry than when praising his brother—I am
thinking of the lines which he wrote on the
departure of his brother from 'a favourite village
in Hampshire'; the lines in which he celebrates
him, with forgivable exaggeration, as

> the Bard who rapture found
> In every rural sight and sound;
> Whose genius warm, and judgement chaste,
> No charm of genuine Nature pass'd;
> Who felt the Muses' purest fires . . .

Joseph Warton and Collins had been boys
together—better still, they had been poets together—at Winchester. At the age of twelve
Collins had written a satire, one phrase [1] of which
he thought sufficiently well of to embody it later
in his *Ode to Evening*. Both he and Warton,
while still at school, had contributed verses to the
Gentleman's Magazine. While still at school they
had been privileged to see Pope. Collins, indeed,
may have seen Pope, not only at Winchester, but
in Chichester—Collins' father, if we may believe
Dr. Johnson, was known in Chichester as 'a hatter

---

[1] 'leathern wing'. But Collins took the phrase originally,
I should suppose, from Shakespeare, *Midsummer Night's Dream*,
II. ii. 4.

of good reputation'; and curious scholarship has
been pleased to note that Pope's friend Caryll,
with whom Pope used to stay in the neighbour-
hood of Chichester, bought his hats from 'Collins'.
Having been poets together at Winchester, Collins
and Joseph Warton continued poets together at
Oxford. Collins was an undergraduate in his
second year when he printed his *Persian Eclogues*.
A MS. note, however, in his own copy of the
book,[1] states that the pieces were 'written at
Winchester School'; and that this is substantially
true (though what was written at Winchester was
no doubt improved at Oxford) I see no reason to
question—the statement is confirmed by Joseph
Warton, who tells us that, for his orientalisms,
Collins drew upon Salmon's *Modern History*.[2] At
a later date Collins used to speak of the poems
as his '*Irish* Eclogues'. But which defects in
them the epithet was meant to hit, I do not know.
Nor, when a great critic, Hazlitt, says that 'parts'
of them are 'admirable', can I guess which these
parts are. The parts of them that are nearest to

[1] Preserved in the Dyce Collection at South Kensington.
It was given by Collins to Joseph Warton when the two
Wartons 'visited him for the last time at Chichester' (MS.
note by Joseph Warton).

[2] London, 3 voll. 4°, 1739. The book was in school use
at Winchester.

interesting are those which emphasize the duty
of poetry (even amatory poetry) to *moralize* :

Well may they please, the Morals of my Song.

It was not long before Collins threw in his lot
with a school of criticism which had for the first
article of its faith the need that there was to make
an end of ' moralizing in verse ', and to substitute
descriptive for didactic poetry ; and he resented
the perversity of criticism which preferred his
Eclogues to his *Odes*.   The *Eclogues*, it is fair to
recall, won the enthusiastic approval of Goldsmith,
who says of them that ' however inaccurate, [they]
excel any in our language '.

Collins was still an undergraduate when he
made his second venture in poetry, with the Verses
' humbly addressed ' to Sir Thomas Hanmer.   Of
this poem Mr. Swinburne censures the ' lack of
critical insight ', while praising its versification as
' generally spirited and competent as well as fluent
and smooth '.   Lines like

Too nicely *Johnson* knew the Critic's Part ;
Nature in him was almost lost in Art

may perhaps be called both good criticism and
competent verse.   On the other hand, when,
addressing Shakespeare, Collins writes

O blest in all that Genius gives to charm,
Whose morals mend us, and whose Passions warm,

I should call the criticism bad and the verse both
incompetent and without spirit.[1]   Perhaps I read
too much undergraduate poetry to be a fair judge ;
but I cannot think Collins' poem worthy either
of himself (his years allowed) or of its occasion.
It was called forth by the first Oxford edition
of Shakespeare.   The occasion was, therefore, an
interesting one.   But it was perhaps spoilt by
Hanmer himself.   Hanmer's Shakespeare is yet
another reminder that the politician who turns
scholar often does so when he has forgotten what
scholarship means.   The reference to ' fumbling
baronets ' in Gray's *Verses from Shakespeare* marks
Gray's sense of Hanmer's merit.

Be that as it may, these two earliest volumes of
Collins had something in them which could please
the taste of the time.   Both volumes were reprinted
during his lifetime.   Yet of the volume of Odes
which he published in 1746, and upon which his
fame rests, no second edition was called for until
after his death.[2]

[1] In a second edition Collins altered the lines, without
improving them.
[2] Of the Odes contained in it, however, three were reprinted
in Dodsley's *Collection*, 1748—the *Ode on the Death of Colonel
Ross*, ' How sleep the brave . . .', and the *Ode to Evening*. The
Ode to Evening was also reprinted in 1753 in Thomas Warton's
The Union : or Select Scots and English Poems.

The volume of Odes bears date 1747; but it in fact appeared in December of the year preceding. In the same month and year appeared Joseph Warton's *Odes on Various Subjects*. The two friends had originally projected a joint volume. ' Being both in very high spirits,' writes Joseph to his brother, ' we took courage, resolved to join our forces, and to publish them (the Odes) jointly.' Why the project fell through is not known.[1] Collins' volume appeared without Preface. Joseph's had a Preface which, if the project of a joint volume had gone through, would have served, we may suppose, to introduce the poetry of both poets. ' The public ', says this Preface, ' has been so much accustomed of late to didactic poetry alone, and essays on moral subjects, that any work where the imagination is much indulged, will perhaps not be relished or regarded. The author, therefore, of these pieces is in some pain, lest certain austere critics should think them too fanciful or descriptive. But he is convinced that the fashion of moralizing in verse has been carried too far, and as he looks upon invention and imagination to be the chief faculties of a poet, so he will be happy if the following Odes may be looked upon

[1] But see below, p. 73.

as an attempt to bring back poetry into its right channel.'

Plainly it is at Pope that ' Fancy's Bard '—so his friends called Joseph Warton—here aims his shaft. The Preface passes for the first critical document of the romantic revival ; and, in the emphasis which it lays upon 'invention and imagination ' as the ' chief faculties of a poet', certainly it anticipates Joseph's later *Essay on the Genius and Writings of Pope*. In the year in which Pope died, Thomas Warton, Joseph's father, had written an *Ode to Taste,* in which Taste, a ' beauteous Queen ' (who reminds us too much of ' Inoculation, heavenly Maid '), Taste, beauteous Queen, is adjured not to leave ' Britannia's Isle ' :

> Since Pope is fled
> To meet his Homer in Elysian Bowers,
> What Bard shall dare resume
> His various-sounding Harp ?
> Let not resistless Dullness o'er us spread
> Deep *Gothic* Night ; for lo ! the Fiend appears,
> To blast each blooming Bay
> That decks our barren Shores.

The notion of Pope meeting his Homer ' in Elysian Bowers ' amused Joseph Warton ; who, some time during the same year, wrote a prose satire, entitled *Ranelagh House* ; in which the

Devil assures Philomides that 'Mr. Pope took his place in the Elysian Fields not among the Poets but the Philosophers, and that he was more fond of Socrates' company than of Homer's'.[1] As for the 'Deep *Gothic* Night' of which his father is apprehensive, it has no terrors for Joseph, who furnishes a rejoinder to the *Ode to Taste* in his *Ode to Fancy*; in which 'let us', he says to Fancy,

Let us with silent footsteps go
To charnels and the house of woe,
To Gothic churches, vaults and tombs,
Where each sad night some virgin comes . . .

and so on—all as naïve and Strawberry-Hillish as you could wish. Nor had Pope been dead many months when Joseph's brother Tom expressed, in a very 'Gothic' piece, *The Pleasures of Melancholy*, a plain preference for Spenser over Pope:

Thro' Pope's soft song tho' all the Graces breathe,
And happiest art adorn his Attic page;
Yet does my mind with sweeter transport glow,
As at the foot of mossy trunk reclin'd,
In magic Spenser's wildly warbled song
I see deserted Una wander wide
Thro' wasteful solitudes and lurid heaths . . .

'Wildly warbled' (a reminiscence of *L'Allegro*)

[1] *Biographical Memoirs of J. Warton*, by Rev. John Wooll, 1806, p. 178.

is sufficiently absurd, no doubt, for the music of
the *Faerie Queene*. So is 'song'—song of any kind
—applied to the verse of Pope ; and the absurdity
is not much mitigated by the circumstance that
Pope's verse had been called 'song' by himself.
But 'wild warblings' were in the air. Even before Pope was in his grave, Joseph Warton had
written, though he had not published, a poem
entitled *The Enthusiast*, in which he had asked—

What are the lays of artful Addison,
Coldly correct, to Shakespeare's warblings wild ?

All these deliverances sufficiently announce a
'programme', a romantic programme ; and parts
of the programme go back, in fact, to Thomas
Warton, the father.

For Thomas Warton, the father, no one will
wish to claim a great place in the history either
of poetry or of criticism. Yet wholly negligible
he certainly is not. Like his younger son, he
was for two successive periods professor of poetry
in the university of Oxford. He was, it is
believed, not a good professor—perhaps, since
he succeeded Trapp, he hardly needed to be.
Isis, however (says Joseph Warton),

placed her ivy on his head,
Chose him, strict judge, to rule with steady reins
The vigorous fancies of her listening swains.

Not content with being a bad professor of poetry
the elder Thomas Warton was also a bad poet.
Not so bad, even so, but that Joseph Warton was
at pains, in 1748, to publish a selection from his
verse. The verse was not good enough to find
a place, later, in Chalmers, or any other of the
Collections ; and until a few months ago I do not
think that any of it had been reprinted. Mr.
Eric Partridge has now printed a sufficient antho-
logy of it, in a volume which contains select
pieces of all three Wartons. He calls his book
The Three Wartons ; and I am tempted to observe
that there was yet a fourth poet in the family—
a sister, Jane Warton. Her merits in poetry
were sufficient to win notice from the Public
Orator at Oxford in the year in which Tom
Warton died. But I do not suppose that they
were greater than that ; and I have not troubled
to hunt her verses through the magazines in
which they took cover. But there was printed
with her father's poems a poem of hers dedicated to his memory. Joseph Warton wrote a
poem on the same theme ; and it is characteristic of him that he preferred his sister's verses
to his own.

Of the father's poems I should be sorry to
call any good. But if Tom Warton wrote nothing

better than the lines on his brother, the father
wrote nothing better—and much a great deal
worse—than the verses addressed to one of his
sons, aged seven months :

> To thee 'tis given to tumble o'er
> Thy absent sire's poetic store
> (With eager hands these lines to seize
> And tear, or lose 'em, as you please)
> Thou too from pedantry art free,
> And I can safely sing to *thee*.

Nothing in truth is more likeable in the Wartons
than the liking that they all have for one another
and for one another's poetry.

One or two of the father's poems possess interest for criticism. Two of them called 'Runic
Odes' perhaps deserve, poor as they are as poetry,
to be called important. They are conjectured to
have stimulated in Gray the wish to naturalize
Scandinavian themes; and no doubt the 'Runic'
curiosity of Tom Warton came to him from his
father. The father's curiosity derives from Temple; who, in his turn, drew on the *Literatura Runica*
of Olaus Wormius. Other pieces of this undis-
tinguished poet are even more interesting—those,
I mean, which betray the influence of Milton's
minor poems. The best of these is, perhaps,
the ode on Ludlow's Cave; but the influence is

felt in other poems as well. Of poets who, in
the earlier part of the eighteenth century, draw
the best of their inspiration from their recollec-
tions of *Il Penseroso*, *L'Allegro*, and *Lycidas*, I am
not sure that Thomas Warton the elder is not
the first in time. Joseph Warton, in 1756, spoke
of the first two of these three poems as being,
until the date when 'they were set to admirable
music by Mr. Handel' (in 1740), almost un-
known—' the private enjoyment of a few curious
readers'; and something to the same effect is to
be found in the Preface to Tom Warton's edition
of the *Poems on several occasions*. The Wartons,
in fact, regarded the minor poems of Milton as
something of a family discovery; and though
their right to do so has recently been challenged,[1]
I am still inclined to think that they knew what
they were talking about. The stimulus was
perhaps supplied by Dryden's *Miscellany*. *Il Penseroso*, *L'Allegro*, and *Lycidas* all found a place in
the *Miscellany* of 1716.[2] This publication, I

[1] G. Sherburn, *The Early Popularity of Milton's Minor
Poems*, 1920. If we may believe Tom Warton, his father was
the means, indirectly, of calling Pope's attention for the first
time to the merits of Milton's minor poems.

[2] Part vi (the second edition). It is interesting, in the
history of the romantic revival, to notice that the volume
contained also the Icelandic *Invocation of Hervor*.

should guess, gave the poems a more extended
vogue than they had enjoyed before. No doubt,
what Joseph Warton says of Handel has also
truth in it. The two younger Wartons, and
Collins and Gray, all came after Handel; and
Handel gave new life in them to an old enthusiasm.[1] But the first enthusiasm came, I suspect,
from Thomas Warton the elder. That he was
well advised, in the zeal of his Miltonizing,
to essay a 'song by Milton left unsung', or unfinished, and write an Ode on the Passion, we
may reasonably doubt. But two others of his
pieces I will mention. He translated Horace's
Bandusian Fountain. So too did Tom Warton
—the son better than the father. Tom used for
his version the metre which Milton had used for
translating the Pyrrha Ode.[2] His father had employed the metre before him, in the *Ode to Taste*
which I have already mentioned. The contest
between father and son is interesting; but yet
more interesting is it that Collins should take
the same metre for his *Ode to Evening*. The
common studies of the Wartons, again, are

---

[1] It is not without significance—especially is it significant
for Collins and Gray—that Handel set to music, in one and the
same year, *Il Penseroso* and Dryden's *Ode on St. Cecilia's Day*.

2 Joseph Warton also used it; and in his *Ode on Shooting*
experimented with a variation on it.

pleasantly illustrated by the circumstance that
all three wrote Odes to Sleep. The best of the
three is Tom Warton's; but it is interesting to
find Joseph Warton taking from his father's Ode
the first three lines of his own without ac-
knowledgement. Whether it was through their
affection for the minor poems of Milton that the
Wartons were led to that zeal for Spenser which
all three of them had, I do not know. That in
these poems especially Spenser was Milton's
'original' they hardly needed Dryden[1] to tell
them. Tom Warton's *Observations upon the Fairie
Queene* nowhere loses relevance from the circumstance that it abounds in Observations upon
the Poems of Milton.

The *Observations* appeared in 1754; and two
years later Joseph Warton published his *Essay
on Pope.* In the history of the romantic revival
these two books are of capital importance. But,
as I have indicated, the 'programme' which they
formulate at leisure is already hinted in the Preface to Joseph Warton's 1746 Odes: the Preface
which, but for an accident, would have introduced also the Odes of Collins. I do not know
that the later *Essay on Pope* adds to the pro-

[1] See the Preface to the *Fables*, Ker's *Dryden*, ii. 247. See
also the Publisher's Advertisement to Milton's *Poems*, 1645.

gramme of the Preface (save a wealth of illustration sometimes tedious) anything material.   But
in the history of poetical theory it is memorable
that the *Essay on Pope* had a good deal of influence
on Wordsworth : the book lay open before him,
if not when he wrote the Preface to *Lyrical Ballads*, at any rate when he wrote the Essay Supplementary to the Preface.   Joseph Warton was
still living when the first edition of *Lyrical Ballads*
was published ; and he had not been dead many
months when the second edition of it appeared.
If he ever saw the book, that poem in it which
pays a well-known tribute to Collins must have
awakened in him interesting memories and re-
flections.   The Essay Supplementary of 1815
mentions Collins as a poet whose poems, utterly
neglected on their first appearance, had become
' universally known '.

If Collins' Odes lacked a Preface, at least they
had a motto ; upon which it would have been
interesting to have Wordsworth's comment.   For
the motto, taken from Pindar, is a Prayer for
Poetic Diction : εἴην εὑρησιεπής—may I be a de-
viser of diction !   It was not for nothing that
Dr. Johnson spoke of Collins as ' seeming to
think that not to write prose is certainly to write
poetry '.   It may be suspected, indeed, that there

was nothing upon which Collins so much prided himself as his diction. The vicious quality of his diction hardly escaped Wordsworth's notice; and our respect for Wordsworth is perhaps not lessened when we observe the power in him to penetrate through so much falsity to what Collins has of true poetic quality.

That Wordsworth used Joseph Warton's *Essay on Pope* is well worth remembering. But so too are some other connexions. It is equally worth remembering that the views expressed in the *Essay on Pope* had not prevented Joseph Warton from translating Vergil into heroic couplets; couplets which are only not to be called Popian because, trying to be like Dryden, they succeed in being like Pitt. It is worth remembering, again, that Tom Warton's *History of English Poetry* falls actually within the lifetime of Wordsworth. When it began to appear, Percy's *Reliques* had been running for a decade. So had Macpherson's *Ossian*; and the forgeries of Chatterton, if they had not been published, were at least ready. Before his *History* was finished—before the third volume of it—Tom Warton may be found playing with theories of a reconciliation between classical and romantic, upbraiding himself as a 'truant from the classic page'. Deepened reflection had

> broke the Gothic chain
> And brought *his* bosom back to truth again.

His sympathies had come over to those who sought

> With arts unknown before to reconcile
> The willing Graces with the Gothic pile.

That was in 1782. Sir Joshua Reynolds, however, to whom the verses were addressed, did
not take this recantation very seriously. ' I may
be allowed ', he writes, ' to entertain some doubts
of the sincerity of your conversion. I have no
great confidence in the recantation of such an old
offender.' Criticism ' may be allowed to entertain some doubts ', not of Warton's conversion,
but of the completeness of his original truancy.
The verses quoted are somewhat like a belated
echo of the verses of a better poet. Nearly fifty
years before, Collins had imaged a similar reconciliation of classical and romantic :

> In *Gothic* Pride it seems to rise !
> Yet *Graecia*'s graceful Orders join,
> Majestic thro' the mix'd Design.

That is said of the Temple of Liberty. But I
fancy that Collins would have been well content
to take the lines as a description of his own
poetry, as an expression of the end which, in

poetry, he and some of his friends sought. The truth is that I conceive the 'romanticism' of Collins and of the Wartons to represent a direction of taste followed with a good deal less of fanatical devotion than sorts with a genuine revolutionary temper. I have no wish, certainly, to belittle the sincerity of that movement of poetry and criticism of which the Wartons were a distinguished part. Yet it is no good pretending that it went deeper than it did. I cannot disguise from myself, first, that it was an Oxford movement; secondly, that it was a Cambridge movement; and thirdly, that it was not a movement in the hearts and minds of men. It was an attempt at a literary revolution, of which the proper precondition was, I feel, lacking—namely, a spiritual revolution. It was preluded, not by the crash of thrones nor by any agonies of a spirit in man dying into life, but by a kind of literary boredom. There was, if I may say so, a change of taste, not a change of heart. The change of taste was something, was much; for latent in it was a sense of the very real distinction that there is between Pope and poetry. But to see through Pope is not necessarily to see into poetry. Nor is that insight, again, to be fetched from antiquarian study. It is a good thing to go

back to Milton and Spenser; a good thing to
tempt curiosity with shadows of the Runic and
the Gothic. But when we have done all that,
and only all that, we are still bookish. I am not
complaining that 1742 was not 1789. But it is
a fact that it was not; and a fact from which
there flow important consequences. 1742 saw
the fall of Walpole; and he made way—for the
Pelhams. 1744 saw the death of Pope; and the
colleges of Oxford and Cambridge began to con-
sider the possibilities of a poetry which should
reconcile the Attic and the Gothic. It was all
very well; but it was all too gentlemanly. You
might hope much from it; but you could not
hope the greatest things.

Nor did the greatest things happen. Nothing
better happened than Collins in Oxford and Gray
in Cambridge.

COLLINS AND GRAY

CRITICISM has always found it hard to love at one and the same time both Gray and Collins. It was easy for Dr. Johnson to disparage both of them in equal degree, and intelligible that he should do so. But writers subsequent to Dr. Johnson have found it hard to praise the one of them without belittling the other. Wordsworth, in his letters,[1] his prefaces, and his poems, has confessed his fondness for Collins. But he would never be persuaded that Gray was a poet at all. His heavy-handed strictures upon Gray's sonnet to the memory of Richard West are well known. 'It will easily be perceived that the only part of this Sonnet which has any value is the lines printed in italics'! The italics are Wordsworth's; but they stamp with 'value' only five lines in all. The offence of the rest is Gray's 'curious elaborateness' in 'poetic diction'. The five good lines are those of which the language

---

[1] See his letter to Dyce, dated 12 Jan. 1829. Mr. Nichol Smith has pointed out to me that the date 1829 is probably a blunder of the editors for 1827—Dyce's edition of Collins appeared in 1827.

'does in no respect differ from that of prose'. A good many persons, none the less, have been obstinate to admire those parts of Gray's poem of which the language is most like the language of poetry. But to Wordsworth even the *Elegy* was 'unintelligible'. 'It has, however,' as Hazlitt says drily, 'been understood.'[1] Mr. Swinburne, again, lavishing on the Odes of Collins the kind of praise that might be thought more proper for the Psalms of David, will not allow any merit to the Odes of Gray—the power and beauty of the *Elegy* he, unlike Wordsworth, recognizes generously. Yet when he has exhausted upon Gray's lyrics all the vocabulary of disparagement, it is a want of humour in him to beg of critics hereafter that they should refrain from the comparison of Gray and Collins altogether; that they should drop a criticism which they can only conduct in a spirit uselessly partisan. Except that Wordsworth and Mr. Swinburne, and some others, have done it badly, I see no reason at all for not comparing these two poets. To compare them is, indeed, the most natural thing in the world. I can see

[1] *Lectures on the English Poets*, VI. But if the reader will consult Coleridge, *Biographia Literaria*, Shawcross, i, p. 26 n., he will see that Hazlitt makes too much of a remark of Coleridge. Coleridge, like Wordsworth, 'thought Collins had more genius than Gray' (*Table Talk*, p. 319, Oxford 1917).

reasons for not comparing Keats and Shelley—
two poets in respect of whom, once again, it
seems to be a rule of criticism to love the one by
depreciating the other. The best reason for not
comparing Keats and Shelley is that they are singularly unlike. They neither invite comparison, nor
reward it. But Gray and Collins do invite comparison.

What ought to be said by any one who com-
pares them can, I believe, be said succinctly.
Personalia are necessarily left on one side. Of
Collins we know next to nothing ; of Gray a great
deal; enough, perhaps, to make us uncomfortable;
certainly too much for it to be easy to fit the *man*
to great poetry, to poetry of the very highest
order. The man is there, and his letters. Gray's
letters, I sometimes feel, are too much flung at
us, too much used to distract us from the im-
partial judgement of his poetry. Gray was an
indolent man ; too indolent for the greatest literature. But his indolence has not paid the proper
penalty. It gave him a wide leisure. He had
time to write letters, and good ones ; letters so
good that, if he had left no poetry, they would
still give him a place in literature. Of Collins
we have only two letters ; till the other day we
had but one.

Gray's literary history—so far as his poetry is concerned—is a very simple one. In 1742 he wrote three Odes of which it is fair to say that they would not to-day be much regarded if he had not written, in 1754, two very much better ones. Of those three Odes I think it the principal glory that, without one of them, the *Hymn to Adversity*, we should not have had Wordsworth's *Ode to Duty*. But the two Odes of 1754, *The Progress of Poesy*, that is to say, and *The Bard*, our literature could ill spare. Both these poems I take to be better verse and better poetry than anything that is to be found in Collins outside his two master poems—I mean, outside the *Ode to Evening* and 'How sleep the brave . . .' On the other hand, until he had read Collins, Gray wrote nothing as good as much that Collins had written. Gray's assimilative faculty was immense: it is hardly to disparage him to say that it was his most distinctive talent; and I have the suspicion that his best owes something to the best of Collins. Even in the *Elegy* he has not disdained to remember Collins' *Ode to Evening*: the second stanza of the *Elegy* plainly echoes the third of the *Ode*.

Be that as it may, Gray was a better scholar than Collins; and when he wrote his two best

Odes he was close on forty. Collins' work is that of a young man of twenty-five, defective both in scholarship [1] and experience. I do not know why, when Collins and Gray are compared, it seems so often to be forgotten that all of Collins that is worth reading (with the exception of a single imperfect piece [2]) proceeds from years matching the years of Keats. I suppose that I must not call Gray, at thirty-eight, middle-aged; albeit we dons grow old before our time. I will merely emphasize, therefore, the maturity of his best work. It is a maturity which might almost be called finality. The best of Gray exhibits immortal perfections—perfections of a kind which

[1] Only bad scholarship, I think, can explain the place which Collins assigns, in his Odes, to the Epode. It needed, again, a bad scholar to suppose that by 'sad Electra's poet' Milton meant Sophocles (see the note on stanza 3 of the *Ode to Simplicity*). It needed a bad scholar to suppose that the poet Alcaeus 'sang the sword' of Harmodius and Aristogiton, who belong to a date something like a century later than Alcaeus. Twice in Collins, again, the scholar will have to stop and ask himself what particular association Sophocles has with Hybla (see *Fear* 34–7, *Simplicity* 13–18).

[2] The *Ode on the Superstitions of the Highlands*. Editors date this Ode '1749', or 'about 1749'. The first quatrain of the eighth stanza looks like an echo of the sixth stanza of Gray's *Elegy*. But this is to be explained by the fact that both Gray and Collins are imitating Thomson (*Seasons: Winter*, 311–17) (who, in turn, depends upon a well-known passage of Lucretius (iii, 894 sqq.)).

are not to be discovered in Collins, even in the best of Collins. Of Collins' poetry the glory resides, not in its perfections, but in its potentialities. These give to it what nothing ever gives, I fancy, to Gray's poetry, an *exciting* quality. Matthew Arnold has said of Gray that 'he never spoke out' in poetry. But I am not at all sure that it is true. I have the sense always, when I read Gray, that he *did* speak out; that he went as far as he could. I never feel that his Odes, with their very special perfections, promise anything greater in their own kind. The perfections of the *Elegy* are more general, and more obvious. But these too seem to me to be very *finished* perfections, and the finality of them to be even a little depressing. They seem, I mean, to end with themselves; to have no forward gaze, no reaching out of hands, no insistence, no cry. The renown of them is fulfilled.

By contrast with all this, it is with 'the inheritors of unfulfilled renown', with Keats, with Chatterton, and, I would even say, with Coleridge,— Coleridge in whom, as in Collins, though under other conditions, the poet died so long before the man,—it is with these that Collins has his place. I wish that we knew as much of him as we know of

Keats, and of Coleridge. With both these poets
his genius and fortune have affinity. Nor is it
easy to divine why we do not know more of him
than we do. The reason is, in part, I suppose,
some nice reticence of his friends; and in part
the circumstance of his apparent failure in poetry.
He is remembered to-day by a book which, while
he lived, nobody read. Nobody was interested
in him until it was too late.

I may raise here a question to which I do not
know the answer. While he lived, Collins, for
whatever reason, less fortunate than Keats or
Chatterton or Coleridge, failed to interest his
contemporaries to the degree which was his due,
failed to catch their imagination. When, in 1763,
Fawkes and Woty published what was, in effect,
the first collected edition of his poems,[1] his best
work, the *Odes*, had been out of print and out
of demand for some seventeen years—all the
copies of the book which he could lay hands
on Collins had himself destroyed. In 1765
appeared Langhorne's edition. This was re-

[1] See above, p. 13 note.

[2] A part of it had appeared in Fawkes and Woty's *Calendar*,
1763 (see below). It is remarkable that, in 1763, only four
years after Collins' death, Johnson supposed him to have been
dead nine years. He repeats the error in 1781; and it is
found in Langhorne, and all editors, until it was corrected by
Dyce in 1827.

printed in 1771 and again in 1781. It was in 1781 that Johnson's *Life* of Collins [2] was published. Six years after Johnson's *Life* of him, Collins' repute stood high enough to induce Foulis of Glasgow to invest him with the dignity of a folio. A year later, his *Ode on the Superstitions of the Highlands* was printed, with a dedication to Joseph and Thomas Warton; and before Joseph died Collins' *Poetical Works* had run into yet three more editions. But to what circumstance, or set of circumstances, we are to attribute the revived interest in Collins—or rather, the first awakening of interest in him—which began four years after his death, and which created a demand for four editions of his Works between 1765 and 1781, I do not know. The interest once roused was likely enough to be sustained; and from 1781 onwards the general direction of literature was sure to favour Collins. But I conjecture that we owe it to the enterprise of Fawkes and Woty that Collins' poetry did not perish altogether. In the bibliographies of Collins nothing is said of Fawkes and Woty's reprint. I can find nothing that connects either of them, personally, with Collins; and I suppose that, when they reprinted his poems in their *Poetical Calendar*, they did so because they had a truer taste in poetry than might have been

expected. That they were somewhat specially
interested in the venture appears sufficiently from
the fact that the twelfth volume of the *Calendar* contains 'Some Account of the Life and Writings of
Mr. William Collins' (pp. 107–12). No other of
their twelve volumes gives any 'Account' of any
of their poets. The first three pages of the Memoir
are written (it is to be inferred) by one, or other, or
both, of the editors of the *Calendar*. But the last
three are supplied 'by a gentleman deservedly eminent in the republic of letters'. The 'gentleman
deservedly eminent' was Johnson. He is not
named; but we must, I think, suppose that these
three pages were known to have been written by
him; and that it was his authority, backing the
enterprise of Fawkes and Woty, which brought
Collins to his true repute. The three pages were
reprinted by Johnson in his *Life* of 1781. If
I am right, they had founded Collins' fame. It
may be that Johnson felt that they had, in fact,
lifted the poetry of Collins to a higher eminence
than was deserved. In any case, he thought it
proper, in 1781, to conclude the *Life* with a paragraph singularly disparaging. For Collins himself he had a genuine affection: 'Collins with
whom I once delighted to converse, and whom I
yet remember with tenderness.' But his last word

upon his poetry is that it belongs to that order which ‘ may sometimes extort praise when it gives little pleasure ’.

Gray, omnivorous, and perhaps a little jealous, in his reading, read, in the month in which they appeared, the Odes both of Collins and of Joseph Warton. ‘ Have you read ’, he asks, ‘ the works of two young authors, a Mr. Warton and Mr. Collins, both writers of Odes ? It is odd enough, but each is the half of a considerable man, and one the counterpart of the other. The first has but little invention, very poetical choice of expression, and a good ear. The second, a fine fancy, modelled upon the antique, a bad ear, great variety of words and images, with no choice at all. They both deserve to last some years, but will not.’ About the last sentence there is something (though, no doubt, it ill becomes me to say so)—something detestably donnish. ‘ I was thirty years old yesterday,’ he goes on. But that is no excuse for being fifty. In general, the criticism is, I think, good : it is as good as it could be, if you admit that it could be good at all when it fails to perceive that Collins and Warton, though part, truly, of a single movement, move in different planes. Warton’s poetry has, upon the whole, those merits which Gray allows to it; and it

has (Warton's own Preface notwithstanding) the
defect that Gray notes—it wants 'invention', or
imagination. About the 'fine fancy' of Collins,
nobody will quarrel; save perhaps to wish at times
that he had cultivated fancy somewhat less, sentiment a great deal more. Nor is 'great variety
of words and images, with no choice at all' really
unfair—not unfair, at any rate, for criticism conveyed by familiar epistle. More interesting, and
more disputable, is what Gray says of Collins'
'bad ear'. There he has Dr. Johnson with him;
who speaks of Collins' lines as being, commonly,
'of slow motion, clogged and impeded with clus-
ters of consonants'. He has Dr. Johnson with
him, a critic so honest that he can never safely be
despised; and he has with him Tennyson, who,
like other poets who have been without ear for
music, had certainly a fine ear in poetry. If
Tennyson's reputation in poetry has not worn so
well as was expected—and with recent attempts
to make him seem again so great a poet as he
was once esteemed I have not much sympathy
—yet as a critic of poetry he has hardly had the
praise he deserves. Tennyson thought the ear
of Gray good, that of Collins (whom none the
less he admired) bad. As an example of Gray's
'wonderful ear' he cited

Though he inherit
Nor the pride nor ample pinion
That the Theban Eagle bear,
Sailing with supreme dominion
Through the azure deep of air

—verses which he spoke of as being 'among the most liquid lines in any language'. 'But what a bad hissing line is that in the poem (of Collins) on the death of Thomson—

The year's best sweets shall duteous rise.'

But it would not be fair to cite the testimony here of Tennyson without remembering that it runs clean counter to that of a poet, his contemporary, who, in the music of verse, was not inferior to him. To Mr. Swinburne Collins was the one poet of his time 'who had in him a note of pure lyric song, a pulse of inborn music irresistible and indubitable . . . The Muse gave birth to Collins; she did but give suck to Gray'. It is, above all, Collins' 'purity of music' which Mr. Swinburne selects for panegyric; and he find in Collins' Odes 'hardly a single false note'. In Gray he is offended everywhere by the 'fanfaronnade and falsetto' of his 'notes'.

These sharply opposed opinions deserve to be set on record. What poets say about other poets

is always interesting ; and ought to be truer than
anything that critics can say.   If, often enough,
it is not, that is perhaps because poets are less
able than other men to escape their own preposses-
sions, and are necessarily more prepossessed.   On
a count of votes, Gray, I should suppose, would
win.   And verbal music is, when all is said and
done, so important an element in poetry that not
to bring matters to the vote is difficult.   It may
be that Gray's music is purer than that of Collins
as being purer of faults ; that the music of Collins
is purer of art, has more of nature and magic.
I am not sure that I believe this.   But it would
explain, if it were true, the conflict of testimony
between Tennyson and Mr. Swinburne.   For myself, I seem to detect in too many of Collins'
notes a too shrilling quality.   Even so, it is easier
to learn art than to learn nature.   Collins might
have lived to learn.   There was little that Gray
could learn—unless it was to forget ; to forget
himself and his perfections.

COLLINS: THE VOLUME OF 1746:
(a) THE EARLIER ODES, AND THE *ODE TO EVENING*

COLLINS' *Odes on Several Descriptive and Allegoric Subjects* is a small quarto volume of fifty-two pages, badly printed, very badly punctuated, and, in respect of its contents, ill arranged. The age was the age of the Indolents. So indolent was Gray that he has missed his place among the great poets. Even Thomas Warton was just sufficiently indolent to miss his place among the great critics. He never cared to finish his *History*; and of what he wrote of it the defects proceed from his fits of indolence. To his own indolence Thomson has erected the pleasantest of memorials. If it be true that, as I seem to remember reading, he was at once so fond of peaches and so lazy in his fondness for them that he ate them from the wall, as they hung, he would seem to have some title to be thought the world's laziest man. So indolent was Collins that you may doubt often whether he re-read what he wrote. He is content to begin a sentence with 'You lov'd her Hills . . .' and go on with 'And turn'd thy Face . . .'[1] He scatters

---

[1] *Ode to Simplicity*, stanza 6.

pronominal adjectives ('his', 'her') in a fashion
which makes indolence scarcely distinguishable
from effrontery, leaving his best stanzas, sometimes, from this cause only, almost unintelligible.
If many of his obscurities come from careless
writing, hardly fewer proceed from careless reading of proofs.   The first stanza of the *Ode on the
Poetical Character* consists of a single sentence of
twenty-two lines ; a conditional sentence, of which
the apodosis is delayed for seventeen lines ; and,
as if this was not bad enough, the whole is
rendered unintelligible by a false punctuation of
the first line (faithfully preserved in, I think, all
the editions save the Pickering edition of 1853).
In addition to that, the first stanza is divided
into two metrical sections, but the third, which
corresponds in its metre, is printed as a single
section—an error which has caused the Ode to
be wrongly classed as 'Pindarique' or 'irregular'.
In the *Ode to Fear*, somewhat similarly, the heading 'Strophe' has been omitted before the first
stanza : though there the error, if it irritates,
does not confuse.   The Strophe of *Mercy*, again,
wants its proper division.   The *Ode to Peace*
betrays by a false catchword[1] that it has been
misplaced ; and, the catchword apart, it quite

[1] p. 40 (1747).

clearly belongs to the series of Odes of patriotic
theme which forms the central section of the
volume of 1746: the continuity of this section is
interrupted by the *Ode to Evening*. The earliest
of the Odes, again, is certainly *The Manners*;
which, however, stands last but one in the book.
This Ode is disfigured by a misprint which,
though it still stands in all the editions, should
hardly have escaped the eye, I will not say of
Collins, but of any proof-reader whom Mr. A.
Millar had handy:

Thou by the Passions nurs'd, I greet
The comic Sock that binds thy Feet !
O *Humour*, Thou whose Name is known
To *Britain*'s favor'd Isle alone.

Be the name of Humour as well known to
Britain's Isle as a poet could wish, is it anywhere
in the world known of Humour that she was ' by
the Passions nurs'd ' ? Quite obviously the *Thou*
of the first of these lines is a misprint for *Tho'*.
It is not the Comedy of Humours, but Collins
himself, who has been nursed by the Passions:
Collins the author of the *Ode on the Passions*,
Collins whose book of Odes opens with poems
addressed to the two essentially tragic passions,
Pity and Fear: Collins who, in delivering him-

self over to Comedy and the Manners, feels the
guilt of a certain truancy.

Some of Collins' friends have left it on record
that he, in fact, was a fastidious corrector; not,
indeed, of his proofs, but of his poems; that he
was forever revising and improving. That is
true, probably, of every poet that ever lived. But
I should think it less true of Collins than of
most; and I suppose it to have been said for the
reason that one or two of his pieces show, in
different editions of them, variants. Yet the
progression of Collins' text, where he altered it,
shows almost always, I fancy, a movement from
a less to a greater carelessness; and this is best
illustrated, perhaps, from what many persons
regard as his best poem. The *Ode to Evening*
exists, as is well known, in two versions; that of
the volume of 1746, and that printed two years
later in Dodsley's *Collection*. In the 1746 version
the eighth stanza of the Ode is given as follows :

> Then let me rove some wild and heathy Scene,
> Or find some Ruin 'midst its dreary Dells,
>   Whose Walls more awful nod
>   By thy religious Gleams.

'Nod' is bad. But Collins often *is* bad; and,
for the rest, the lines make sense and give a

picture. The same cannot be said of the Dodsley version, the later, and, as it is commonly esteemed, the better version :

Then lead, calm Vot'ress, where some sheety lake
Cheers the lone heath, or some time-hallow'd pile,
 Or upland fallows grey
 Reflect it's last cool gleam.

The late Professor Ker, in a lecture upon *Some Romantic Fallacies,*[1] has a comment upon these two versions which is not a little mysterious to me. To him the Dodsley version is so much better than that of 1746 as to be, in itself, 'significant for the progress of the romantic movement' :

'In the second version,' he writes, 'besides the true personification in "votaress", who is from Milton's *Maske,* there is the fresh vision and understanding of the effect of a surface of water in twilight, when all the land round it is dark, and in place of the conventional ruin that "nods", there is the old building, church or castle, dimly seen as part of the evening light along with the large bulging hill-side. If you look into it, you will see at once that the water is to the west, the "time-hallow'd pile" to the east, and all this is given in the fewest words, and with no vanity or insistence on the accurate rendering. The romantic fallacy is cleared away, and its place is taken in a different mode of vision and poetry.'

[1] *The Art of Poetry,* pp. 86–7.

Here, of the sentence which begins 'If you look into it . . .', I feel obliged to say that, look into it as I will, I can see, of all that Ker sees, nothing. To be frank, I have no idea what he means. What matters more is that, leaving Ker, and going back to Collins himself, I have no idea what Collins means. Of this second version I can discover, in fact, neither the meaning nor the grammar. I had at one time thought that it would be possible to make sense of it by reading, for 'it's last cool gleam', in the last line of it, ' *Light's* last cool gleam '. [1] But even if that emendation were a true one, I know that no one would think it so; and I should be told that it was not my business to re-write Collins. Indeed, it is so far not my business to re-write Collins that it was the business of Collins himself; and in fact he undertook it. But he brought to it, not revising care, but a new carelessness. He re-wrote his stanza. But did he re-read what he had re-written ?

I have dwelt on these bibliographical trivialities (if they are trivialities) in order to make plain that, when he published his Odes, Collins took less than ordinary care to make

[1] I find that M. Émile Legouis long since conjectured ' thy ' for ' it's '; and this may well be right.

his book such a book as might be read with
pleasure.

If Collins had a bad printer, he had a bold one.
Mr. A. Millar was bold to print as many as 1,000
copies of the *Odes*. For the *Persian Eclogues* an
edition of 500 copies had sufficed. How many
copies Collins destroyed, in what Mr. Swinburne
calls his ' fever-fit of angry despair ', can only be
guessed. But the book is now a rare one—a
copy of it, it is interesting to note, ' extremely
rare ', figured in the catalogue of Wordsworth's
books when these were sold in 1859.[1] It has,
however, been recently reprinted in facsimile by
Mr. Noel Douglas; and the reprint may well
do something to promote a more careful study
of Collins than is, I fancy, common. Of how
many of the poems in it, I sometimes wonder,
could the average student of poetry give so much
as the names—leaving aside the three pieces which
the anthologists have saved out of ' the iniquity
of oblivion ' ? I have noticed already that the
central section of the book consists of a series of
five patriotic Odes. One of these is, in length,
the most considerable by far of all Collins' Odes.
Yet how many persons have ever thought of
Collins as a patriotic poet ?

[1] E. Morley, *Correspondence of Crabb Robinson*, ii, p. 872.

I have said that the arrangement of the book
is bad. The earliest of the poems in it is the
last but one. Very few of the Odes are dated
or certainly dateable. But the Ode entitled *The
Manners* is, on the face of it, a farewell to university studies by an undergraduate just 'going
down': I fancy that the opening of it was written
with conscious reminiscence of Vergil's ' Ite hinc,
inanes, ite . . .' In it Collins bids farewell to
Oxford and Oxford philosophy. Philosophy was
' for clearer ken design'd ; and his ' silent search '
has ' in vain requir'd ' her truths. He has made
a failure of philosophic study, which he has felt
to be too far removed from practical life, too
much ' from Action's Paths retir'd '. If ever he
makes a return upon Philosophy, it will be, not
in the pure spirit of science, but with the hope to
conquer, by the aid of philosophy, the Passions
and the Follies. The personal touch is pleasantly
intriguing. ' A poet ', says one of Collins' editors,
' a poet, and not to have felt the tender passion,
would be a creature which the world has never
yet seen.' He tells us, accordingly, that at some
time not specified, but which may well be the
time of *The Manners*, ' Collins was extremely fond
of a young lady . . . who did not return his
affections '. The young lady, in fact, preferred

soldiers to scholars. There were wars to be won;
and she engaged herself to a Colonel Ross, a
gallant soldier who fell in the battle of Fontenoy.
It was to the memory of this Colonel Ross that
Collins, with a poet's generosity, dedicated the
Ode which bears Ross' name in its title. It is a
poor poem. But out of it grew subsequently the
most perfect of all Collins' poems, the lines which
begin 'How sleep the brave . . .'. Whether the
lady was ranked by Collins, when he wrote *The
Manners*, as among his Passions or his Follies, it
is perhaps more interesting to guess than to know.
He bids farewell to Philosophy; and determines
to give himself to the observation of social manners, of the human comedy:

Thy walks, *Observance*, more invite.

Observance grates. But the poem, down to line
30, is good and spirited; in its own kind as
good as anything that Collins wrote. I have the
suspicion that it would have been worth his while
to have essayed oftener this lighter kind; just as
I suspect that Joseph Warton, if he had oftener,
that is to say, more than once, essayed satire,
would have done well with it.[1] The conclusion

[1] I do not know that anything in his serious verse improves
on these lines (from the Satire, *Fashion*):

O France, whose edicts govern dress and meat,
Thy victor, Britain, bends beneath thy feet!

of the poem invokes 'Nature boon', in whose guidance the youthful Collins proposes to see life :

> The *Sports* and I this Hour agree
> To rove the sceneful World with Thee !

There you have (and it is well, perhaps even pleasant, to remember him) the Collins who (if we may believe Gilbert White) 'threw up his demyship and, going to London, commenced a man of the town, spending his time in all the dissipation of Ranelagh, Vauxhall, and the play-houses'; the Collins who, according to another friend, Mr. Ragsdale, went about London 'gaily dressed, with a feather in his hat', presenting an appearance 'by no means that of a young man who had not a single guinea he could call his

> Strange, that pert grasshoppers should lions lead,
> And teach to hop and chirp across the mead !
> Of fleets and laurell'd chiefs let others boast,
> Thy honours are to bow, dance, boil and roast.
> Let Italy give mimic canvass fire,
> Carve rock to life, or tune the lulling lyre ;
> For gold let rich Potosi be renown'd,
> Be balmy-breathing gums in India found :
> 'Tis thine for sleeves to teach the shantiest cuts,
> Give empty coxcombs more important struts,
> Prescribe new rules for knots, hoops, manteaus, wigs,
> Shoes, soups, complexions, coaches, farces, jigs.

This spirited variation of the Vergilian *Excudent alii* ought, I think, to be better known than it is.

own'; the Collins who 'had the liberty of the
scenes and of the greenroom'. Mr. Ragsdale
adds, it is fair to say, that our poet 'made diverting observations on the vanity and consequence
of that class of people', to wit, the floating popu-
lation of greenrooms. It is a pity that some of
these diverting observations have not survived.

This earliest of Collins' Odes, then, has about
it something of the spirit of the years to which it
belongs. How long, or to what degree, Collins
indulged 'the liberty of the greenroom' we do
not know. His father, the 'hatter of good reputation', had wished to make a gentleman of
him, or at least a clergyman. But 'by a wealthy
tobacconist of Fleet Street' Collins was induced
to abandon the idea of taking orders. I would
give much to know a little more of this wealthy
and, we must suppose, worldly tobacconist. The
inconsequence of the connexions has something
that puts one in mind of Coleridge. It is thought
that Collins entertained at this time the project
of writing for the stage. If he did not, it does
not matter; but if he did, he set about it in the
best way possible (so I should suppose). He
undertook a translation of Aristotle's *Poetics*. For
his translation he was paid in advance. Later he
preferred to return the money. The Aristotle

was just one of those grandiose beginnings of which, like Coleridge again, he was prodigal. Not long after, he was busy projecting a History of the Revival of Learning. Something, however, did come of the Aristotle. For to Collins' pre-occupation with the *Poetics* we owe, it can hardly be doubted, the two poems which stand first in the volume of 1746—the Odes addressed to Pity and Fear. Collins' Pity and Fear are, I have already said, the Pity and Fear of Aristotle: personi-fications of the two essentially tragic Passions. Neither Ode can rank high as poetry. But the *Ode to Pity* is interesting for the reference in its fourth stanza to the tragedies of Otway;[1] and again for the circumstance that the fifth stanza of it was suggested by a poem written by Joseph Warton when he was still at school.[2] The metre of the Ode is the same as that of the *Ode to Peace* and the lines on Colonel Ross: the old six-line 'romance' stanza, as it is sometimes called. Its uses in English poetry had been various. In the fourteenth century it was a hymn metre as well

---

[1] A reference, however, not very felicitously managed. The 'Wren' that figures in the first two lines of it carries obscure credentials:

> There first the Wren thy Myrtles shed
> On gentlest Otway's infant Head.

[2] T. Warton, *The Reaper*, No. 26.

as a ballad metre. Both Warton and Akenside use it for Ode. When they do so, they are perhaps not worse poets than in other metres. But Collins in this metre is always infelicitous; at least he is always below his best.

Of the *Ode to Fear*, the concluding lines seem to announce in Collins the ambition of tragic poetry. But more interesting, perhaps, is that stanza of it which hints that his mind is already dwelling on patriotic themes. Speaking of Aeschylus, Collins recalls that that great artist in tragic fear fought at Marathon :

> For not alone he nurs'd the Poet's flame,
> But reach'd from Virtue's Hand the Patriot's
> Steel.

Patriotic themes constitute, as I have already noticed, the most considerable single section of the volume of 1746.

These two Odes were clearly written as a pair. If their titles did not sufficiently say so, that is said in the last lines of the Epode to *Fear*:

> Tho' gentle *Pity* claim her mingled Part,
> Yet all the Thunders of the Scene are thine !

That they belong to Collins' earliest work follows, I think, from what I have already said ; and I suppose their place in the book to point in the same direction. Strictly, *The Manners* should

have stood first.   But that is placed where it is
for no better reason than the desire to juxtapose
The Manners and *The Passions*—of the reason why
The Passions comes last I will say something
presently.   *Fear* is the first of Collins' Græcizing
Odes.   It has the strophic form which he affects
in these Odes, with the Epode interposed between
strophe and antistrophe.   The printer, or Collins
himself, has forgotten to label the strophe ; and
the circumstance that the strophe has 25 lines,
the antistrophe 26, seems to be explained by supposing that a line has been accidentally lost either
before or after line 9 (which wants its proper
rhyme).   Lines 7–8 of the antistrophe, again,
match decasyllables against the elsewhere pre-
vailing octosyllables.[1]   But the scholar and the
average reader alike will readily credit this to
design and not to accident.   The Græcizing
character of the Ode hardly, in any case, goes
beyond this somewhat rudimentary essay in
strophic structure.   The verse of the Epode is
the old elegiac stanza ; that of the strophe and
antistrophe the infinitely older octosyllabic couplet,
the verse of *Il Penseroso* (echoes of Milton will
be easily detected).

[1] Lines 7–8 of the strophe are six-syllabled, and there is the
corresponding shortening in the antistrophe.

I have pointed out how the *Ode to Fear* prepares the way for the patriotic Odes. But the pair of Odes which *Pity* and *Fear* give is separated from the section of patriotic poems by another pair, the *Ode to Simplicity* and the *Ode on the Poetical Character*. Of these two Odes, again, the first follows the Latin pattern of Odes; the second has just as much and just as little of Greek form as the *Ode to Fear*. Collins has forgotten to label the three stanzas of this second Ode; and the printer has destroyed the true paragraphing. But the first 22 and the last 22 lines correspond as strophe and antistrophe, and stanza 2 is what Collins supposed an Epode to be. Both Odes contain better poetry than anything of Collins which had preceded them. And for a good reason. The first of them is written in a metre of Milton—each of its nine stanzas is metrically equivalent to the first six lines of the stanza in which Milton's *Nativity Hymn* is written; while the second of them, the *Ode on the Poetical Character*, is, in effect, an Ode on the poetical character of Milton.

The *Ode to Simplicity* has been, I think, a good deal overrated. It opens, it is true, with five stanzas which are as good, or nearly as good, as

Collins' best; and throughout, the rhythms are
managed with fine feeling. The end of the first
stanza is less good, certainly, than the rest of
it, and barely escapes obscurity. The epithet
'Thymy', in the third stanza—perhaps taken from
Thomson—[1] displeases; so does 'wavy', in the
fourth ('wavy' is used again in the *Ode to Evening*); but better poets have done worse in the
same kind. The third stanza creates troubles
for scholarship, upon which I have sufficiently
remarked in a note, earlier. Even so, these first
five stanzas have a real, and perhaps individual,
beauty. It is in the three stanzas that follow
them that the real failure of power shows itself.
And having said so, I had better set them out:

6

While *Rome* could none esteem
But Virtue's Patriot Theme,
You lov'd her Hills, and led her Laureate Band:
But staid to sing alone
To one distinguish'd Throne,
And turn'd thy Face, and fled her alter'd Land.

7

No more, in Hall or Bow'r,
The Passions own thy Pow'r,
Love, only Love her forceless Numbers mean:

[1] *Liberty*, ii, 139.

For Thou hast left her Shrine,
Nor Olive more, nor Vine,
Shall gain thy Feet to bless the servile Scene.

8

Tho' Taste, tho' Genius bless,
To some divine Excess,
Faints the cold Work till Thou inspire the
whole;
What each, what all supply,
May court, may charm our Eye,
Thou, only Thou can'st raise the meeting Soul!

As one of the especial virtues of Collins Mr. Swinburne has mentioned 'clarity of style'; as among
the sins that too easily beset him, Dr. Johnson
has mentioned 'harshness and obscurity'. They
cannot both be right; and how wrong Mr. Swinburne is the stanzas I have quoted sufficiently
indicate. If there is 'clarity of style' here, I do
not know what words mean. The obscurity of
the sixth stanza I can best illustrate by para-
phrasing it. The first three lines of it do not
mean (what they say) that while Rome was not
able to esteem anybody (i. e. any*thing*) except
patriotic poetry, Simplicity loved the hills of Rome.
They mean that so long as Rome was content
with her native Roman virtues, so long did Simplicity love her hills and direct her poets. (I feel
the forced character of this interpretation. Yet the

poets in whom Rome was particularly interested
were not, as Collins' language seems to suggest,
the epic poets, but, as appears immediately, the
poets of pastoral).   Accordingly, Simplicity

> staid to sing alone
> To one distinguish'd Throne,

—which should mean that she stayed to sing in
solitude to one 'distinguish'd' (or renowned)
throne, or monarch; but which does, in fact,
mean that she only, or merely ('alone'), stayed
to sing to the one throne, or monarch, whom
she was pleased so to distinguish from the rest.
She did not stay beyond the reign of Augustus.
Such minor blemishes in this stanza as 'You
lov'd her Hills . . . And turn'd thy Face' I am
content to pass by uncommenting (this particular
solecism I have already mentioned).

The seventh stanza presents, so far as I can
discover, no difficulty at all to any of Collins'
editors.   They all know by nature what I won to
only by prayer and fasting : that 'her' in the third
line stands for 'Rome's'.   At one time I had
given it up.   I had supposed this impossible 'her'
to have crept into the text from the line following, displacing some quite different word.   And,
waxing frantic, I had re-written the whole verse—

Love, only Love, *shrills* forceless Numbers mean:

(supposing *mean* to be, not a verb, but an adjective). But it will never do; and we must take what we are given. We must suppose Collins to say that no longer in hall or bower do the Passions own the authority of Simplicity; Rome's forceless numbers mean only Love (i.e. the Roman poets are interested, so feeble are they, only in amatory poetry).

> For Thou hast left her Shrine,
> Nor Olive more, nor Vine,
> Shall gain thy Feet to bless the servile Scene.

Simplicity has left Rome's shrine—which seems to mean merely that she has left Rome, though the 'Shrine' might more naturally be taken to be Love's shrine; and olive and vine, i.e. bucolics and georgics, pastoral poetry in any of its forms, can no longer tempt Simplicity to bless, or grace with her presence, a Rome which the successors of Augustus have reduced to slavery, to a 'servile Scene'.

Langhorne hazards the opinion that in the last lines 'the writings of the Provençal poets are principally alluded to'.[1] And for some such allusion 'Hall or Bow'r' seems to prepare us. But the jump from Augustus to the troubadours is a

---

[1] The suggestion may perhaps be supported by a comparison of the lines with lines 53 sqq. of the Epistle to Hanmer (ed. i).

veritable *salto mortale* ; nor is it easy to say why the
fact that Simplicity has left *Rome* should weaken
her control of the Passions in the medieval Hall
or Bower.   The truth is, as I think, that no ingenuity can adjust the hang of these two stanzas,
nor acquit Collins here of that imperfect control
of thought which his writing often exhibits.

In the eighth stanza, the ' meeting Soul ' of the
last line is sufficiently obscure ; and I do not know
that the obscurity of it is altogether excused by
its derivation from Milton's *L'Allegro*.   In the
same stanza,

> Tho' Taste, tho' Genius bless,
> To some divine Excess

can be imputed, I am tempted to say, neither to
taste nor to genius in Collins.   *Taste* recalls the
elder Thomas Warton's ode to that deity.   But
the ' divine Excess ' spoken of sorts with the
function only of genius, not of Taste—who has
no excesses.   In the line that follows ' the *cold*
Work ' is such as might be expected, certainly,
from mere taste, but matches ill with the idea
either of genius or of ' divine Excess '.   We feel
Collins to be losing his drift ; and we are not in
any degree reassured when we reach lines 4–5 :

> What each, what all supply,
> May court, may charm our Eye.

We were speaking of what Taste and Genius supply to *poetry*; and not the eye, but the ear, is in question.

The last stanza of the Ode has a personal interest. Of these, says Collins—of Taste, that is, and Genius—let others ask aid :

> Of these let others ask,
> To aid some mighty Task,
> I only seek to find thy temperate Vale :
> Where oft my Reed might sound
> To Maids and Shepherds round,
> And all thy sons, O *Nature*, learn my Tale.

Here, I would notice in passing, that Simplicity is, in the last line, called plainly 'Nature', who in the first line of the first stanza was merely said to be taught by Nature, and who has been treated throughout as though there were no other nature but natural poetry. The conclusion seems to announce Collins' intention to devote himself hereafter wholly to pastoral poetry, in one or other of its several kinds. There is no hint more of the ambition of tragic poetry, nor of any kind of heroic verse. It is in pastoral that Collins hopes to find his true field. And what kind of pastoral, the Ode that follows puts beyond doubt. In the *Ode on the Poetical Character* Collins describes himself as withdrawing from love-poetry—upon

which, indeed, we did not know him to have been
engaged, but we may take his word for it.   He
retreats from ' *Waller's* Myrtle Shades ', and views

> that Oak, the fancied [1] Glades among,
> By which as *Milton* lay, His Ev'ning Ear,
> From many a Cloud that drop'd Ethereal Dew,
> Nigh spher'd in Heav'n its native Strains could
> hear.

Milton's 'Ev'ning Ear' is bad; nor does only
one act of thought suffice to assure us that ' its ',
in the last line, refers back, neither to Cloud, nor
to Dew, nor to Heav'n, but to the ' Ev'ning Ear '.
The 'Ev'ning Ear' and the oak together (the
oak, quite obviously, ' th' accustom'd Oke' of
Il Penseroso 60) tell us plainly what order of pastoral Collins is meditating.   Perhaps, indeed, medi-
tation has already reached accomplishment.   For
if Collins had known how to arrange his book,
there should have followed directly upon this
Ode a better and more famous one.   The oak and
'fancied Glades' and 'Ev'ning Ear' prepare us for
better strains than their own ; they prepare us for

> If ought of Oaten Stop, or Pastoral Song,
> May hope, chaste Eve, to soothe thy modest Ear,
> Like thy own solemn Springs,
> Thy Springs, and dying Gales . . .

[1] The editions of Mr. Stone and Mr. Poole both have, by
a bad misprint, *fanciest*.

It is to pastoral of this order that the *Ode on the
Poetical Character* points; and we may well think
that Collins judged truly where his best powers
lay.

If the *Ode to Simplicity* has been somewhat overrated, that on the Poetical Character has, I think,
not received the praise which it deserves.[1] A
good deal of it is almost absurdly faulty. It
opens badly. The first stanza of it, interesting
for the reference, in its first lines (prosaic as
these are), to 'that gifted Bard', Spenser, is cum-
brously constructed, and none too perspicuous.
It consists, as I have mentioned already, of a
single sentence, twenty-two lines in all, with the
main verb emerging on a forlorn hope at line 20.
Yet the second stanza, at least, of this Ode hints
powers of a high order. Just as the magic cestus
of Florimel in the *Faerie Queene* might be worn by

> One, only One, unrival'd Fair,

so the Magic Band of Poetry can be assumed
only by him for whom it is predestined:

The Band, as Fairy Legends say,
Was wove on that creating Day,
When He, who call'd with Thought to Birth, 25
Yon tented Sky, this laughing Earth,

---

[1] Except from Hazlitt: see below, pp. 120, 122–3.

And drest with Springs, and Forests tall,
And pour'd the Main engirting all,
Long by the lov'd *Enthusiast* woo'd,
Himself in some Diviner Mood,   30
Retiring, sate with her alone,
And plac'd her on his Saphire Throne,
The whiles, the vaulted Shrine around,
Seraphic Wires were heard to sound,
Now sublimest Triumph swelling,   35
Now on Love and Mercy dwelling;
And she, from out the veiling cloud,
Breath'd her magic Notes aloud:
And Thou, Thou rich-hair'd Youth of Morn,
And all thy subject—Life—was born! [1]   40
The dang'rous Passions kept aloof,
Far from the sainted growing Woof:
But near it sate Ecstatic *Wonder*,
List'ning the deep applauding Thunder:
And *Truth*, in sunny Vest array'd,   45
By whose the Tarsel's Eyes were made;
All the shad'wy Tribes of *Mind*,
In braided Dance their Murmurs join'd,
And all the bright uncounted *Pow'rs*
Who feed on Heav'n's ambrosial Flow'rs.   50

There are characteristic obscurities here.   But
the birth of the Poet from the union of Fancy
and the Father of all things is audaciously conceived, and ornamented with rich and sounding
phrase.   If the opening hangs a little, that is due

[1] I have corrected the punctuation of line 40.

to the negligence which has allowed the subject, 'He', of line 25 to wait till line 31 for the verb which he is destined to govern ('sate'). The 'rich-hair'd Youth of Morn', in line 39, has caused difficulty to Mrs. Barbauld,[1] who supposes him to be the Sun. But clearly he is the Poet, who has the rich, or long, hair of all poets, and of Apollo, father of poets. The boldness of all the imagery is surprising, is almost astonishing. To Mrs. Barbauld (and to some later editors) it gives acute offence. 'This strange and by no means reverential fiction concerning the Divine Being', she says. Some of the right things about Mrs. Barbauld have been said already by Wordsworth; and I pass her by. But I am not sure whether either Shelley or Keats, certainly not Milton or Wordsworth, would have ventured to conceive God himself as wooed 'by the lov'd Enthusiast', Fancy; to speak of God as 'Himself in some Diviner Mood' retiring and sitting alone with Fancy; of Fancy seated on the Sapphire Throne—to Collins, the Throne of God; in Milton, the Sapphire Throne is the throne of Christ.

The ode ends disappointingly; the conclusion of it affords yet another illustration of Collins'

[1] Prefatory Essay, p. xxiv, 1802.

imperfect control of his own connexions. It is idle, he says, to strive to-day to emulate Milton:

In vain—Such bliss to One alone,
Of all the Sons of Soul was known,
And Heav'n, and *Fancy*, kindred Pow'rs,
Have now o'erturn'd th' inspiring Bow'rs,
Or curtain'd close such Scene from ev'ry future
View.

'Heav'n, and *Fancy*, kindred Pow'rs' seems to forget the espousal and marriage of God to 'the lov'd Enthusiast', Fancy—to forget it, or to weaken it pitifully; while the ascription to Heaven and Fancy, and not to Pope and Taste, of the act by which 'th' inspiring Bow'rs' (an uninspiring jargon!) are 'o'erturn'd' is ill conceived and disconcerting. Even so this Ode has passages equal to the best of Collins; and even where it is least successful it is interesting.

Upon it follow, or were meant to follow,[1] the five patriotic Odes. But between the fourth and fifth of them Collins has interposed the *Ode to Evening*. If he had known how to arrange his book, he would, as I said, have placed the *Ode to Evening* immediately after those strains of the *Ode on the Poetical Character* which prelude it. I will be more helpful to the reader than Collins

[1] See above, pp. 46-7, 66.

cared to be; and I will say here of the *Ode to Evening* what I have to say.

This is commonly accounted Collins' most perfect composition. I agree with Mr. Swinburne in thinking it a better poem than *The Passions*, which some persons have preferred to it. But I wish that Mr. Swinburne would not always say too much. 'As surely', he writes, 'as surely as, for instance, the *Ode to Duty* is a work of greater perfection and more perfect greatness than that *On the Intimations of Immortality*, the Ode on the Passions is a work of less equal elevation and purity of excellence than, for example, is the *Ode to Evening*'. The truth is that the *Ode to Duty* is a poem very much inferior to the Immortality Ode—at once less greatly perfect and less perfectly great. But that does not prevent Mr. Swinburne being right when he prefers the *Ode to Evening* to *The Passions*. Even so, 'equal' in its 'elevation' the poem is not, nor, I think, pure in its excellence. If there is to be talk of 'perfection', for my part, I should give the palm, among Collins' poems, to 'How sleep the brave . . .'. That it is a better poem than the *Ode to Evening*, I do not say. Only that it is a more perfect one. To this I shall return.

The *Ode to Evening* is written in a stanza

invented by Milton ; it is written in the metre which Milton used for his version of Horace's ' Quis multa gracilis te puer in rosa . . .'. It was used by all three of the Wartons ; but between Milton and Collins by no one else, I believe. If it has been used since Collins, examples of it have escaped me.[1] If it has not, I cannot sufficiently marvel why ; for, except perhaps to Thomas Warton the elder, it has brought luck to every one who has tried it. Collins has taken Milton's metre ; moved thereto, no doubt, by the example of the Wartons. But he has taken from Milton much else besides his metre. If the diction of the poem is purer than Collins' diction mostly is, that is because so great a part of it is derived from Milton. I know no poem so beautiful or so famous of which the diction is in an equal degree derivative. I say that, not in disparagement ; but quite the contrary. It is proper to mark that Collins never found an individual manner. Nor, till just the end, did Keats. Collins did not live to find and fix his own style and language. But he came near enough to make us sure that he had it in him to do so. That he should discover an

---

[1] Mr. Frederick Page has called my attention to the fact that the metre is used by Kirke White (twice) and by Sara Coleridge.

individual style, nothing could hinder save unkind fate—the fate that froze at their marvellous source all his mortal powers : the fate harder than dying.

Both Collins and Joseph Warton had prepared, for one and the same volume, separate Odes to Evening. That there was overlapping, here and elsewhere, furnishes a part-reason, it may be, why the project of a joint volume was dropped. Warton's Ode is a poor thing. But the two Odes were hardly written in complete independence of one another—that is plain on a superficial comparison of them ; and we happen to know that Warton's was written first.[1] Collins' first stanza invokes 'chaste', or 'pensive', Eve, who is invoked, in the first stanza of Warton, as 'meek-eyed maiden '—in line 42 of Collins' poem she is 'meekest *Eve* '. Both poets, in their second stanza, pass to the sinking of the sun :

When Phoebus sinks beneath the gilded hills, says Warton. Collins, more amply, has

> while now the bright-hair'd Sun
> Sits in yon western Tent, whose cloudy Skirts,
>   With Brede ethereal wove,
>   O'erhang his wavy Bed.

We have met 'wavy' before, without liking it. But the description of the 'bright-hair'd Sun'

---

[1] See Dyce's edition of Collins, 1827, p. 184.

K

sitting in a Tent of which the *Skirts* overhang his
Bed is perhaps worse—in its accurately calculated
infelicity. In Warton's third stanza, the Dryads
come forth in 'evening dance' among the dews.
Collins keeps them for his sixth and seventh
stanzas; making of them Elves and Nymphs and
Hours, whose office is to prepare amid 'freshening
Dews' the shadowy Car of Eve. I doubt, again,
whether Collins' beetle with 'heedless hum' does
not echo distantly the 'hoarse hummings of un-
numbered flies' in Warton's poem. The first two
lines, once more, of Warton's last stanza,

O modest Evening, oft let me appear
A wandering votary in thy pensive train,

are recalled by more than one phrase of Collins.
Warton's 'pensive train' of Evening is father to
the 'shrinking Train' of 'pensive *Eve*' in Collins.
His 'modest Evening' gave to Collins' 'chaste
Eve' her 'modest Ear'; and his 'wandering votary'
has wandered into Collins' 'calm Vot'ress'. (In
Collins the votaress is the goddess herself, in
Warton the votary is the poet.)

There are these suggestions of dependency,
individually thin and distant, but cumulatively,
I fancy, not negligible. It is fair, however, to
note that three of these coincidences would not
exist if the Dodsley version of Collins' poem were

not extant. The 'Vot'ress', and the 'modest' Ear of 'pensive' Eve, come from the Dodsley revision.

Considered structurally, Collins' Ode falls into three main divisions. The first of these is given by lines 1–20; in which, if 'Pastoral Song' has any power to soothe Eve's 'modest Ear', the poet asks that goddess to teach him 'to breathe some soften'd Strain', sorting with the stillness of the hour. By 'some softened strain' he means, no doubt, a strain soft in comparison with his normal odic manner, the manner, say, of *The Passions*, or the Odes to Fear and Liberty. When this prayer, and the first division of the poem, ends, the poet has in a sense said all that he had to say. At least, few readers, I fancy, can fail to feel that the connexion of these first twenty lines with the twenty lines which make the second division of the poem is ill managed. 'For when thy folding Star', Collins goes on, when, that is, the evening star, rises, and Eve's ministers get ready her 'shadowy Car'—

Then let me rove some wild and heathy Scene,
Or find some Ruin 'midst its dreary Dells . . .

The 'Gothic' wildness and dreariness jars here, I feel, upon the quiet of what has preceded. This feeling is intensified when I pass to the next

stanza, in which the poet anticipates that 'blus-
t'ring winds' (deriving from *Paradise Lost*, ii, 286)
may keep him from wandering over the wild and
heathy scene and the dreary dells—and compos-
ing the while, we must suppose, his 'soften'd
Strain'.   If that be so, he prays for a mountain
hut from which he can 'view Wilds and swelling
Floods'.   Having said so much, and having failed
to achieve, I feel, true harmony between what he is
saying and what he has already said, he adds, in his
third division, a kind of epilogue.   In Spring, he
says, in Summer, and

> While sallow *Autumn* fills thy Lap with Leaves,
> Or *Winter* yelling thro' the troublous Air,
>   Affrights thy shrinking Train,
>   And rudely rends thy Robes,

—all of this, be it noted, marring the note of quiet
on which he began, and on which he is going to
end—through all the length of all these periods,
he says (however boisterous they be),

> So long regardful of thy quiet Rule,
> Shall *Fancy*, *Friendship*, *Science*, smiling *Peace*,
>   Thy gentlest Influence own,
>   And love thy fav'rite Name.

The 'fav'rite Name' is kept a secret—is it
'chaste' or 'modest' or 'pensive'?   Or is the
'fav'rite Name' of Evening just Evening, as I

suspect? I will not pretend to say; and I am concerned only to notice the manner in which '*Winter* yelling', the 'shrinking Train' of Eve, and her rudely rent robes, jar with the 'quiet Rule' of that goddess. It is true that the Dodsley version, for 'regardful of thy quiet Rule', offers 'sure-found beneath the sylvan shed'. But that does not heal the discord, for it leaves the immediately following 'gentlest Influence' untouched. 'Sure-found beneath the sylvan shed' refers back, we must suppose, to the mountain hut to which, in stanza 9, the poet has announced his intention of retiring in bad weather. But what '*Fancy, Friendship, Science*, smiling *Peace*' are doing in the sylvan shed, or how they strayed into the poem at all, seems past finding out.

The diction of the poem is, as I have said, and for the reason I have given, purer than that which Collins mostly commands. Every now and again, however, against a phrase either artfully or naturally adapted from Milton, there jostles some eighteenth-century triviality:

> Or where the Beetle winds
> His small but sullen Horn,
> As oft he rises 'midst the twilight Path,
> Against the Pilgrim born in heedless Hum.

The first two lines are *Lycidas*: the 'twilight

Path' is Collins, is eighteenth-century; so is the
tiresome 'Pilgrim' of the last line, who is only,
in plain English, a man out for a walk. The
obscurity of this last line is Collins' own—I suppose 'born' is for 'borne'; but it takes more
ingenuity to determine whether it is the Beetle or
the Pilgrim that is 'born in heedless Hum'.

This sort of analysis is, I am sensible, too
little humane in a material of such delicacy and
grace.   But I had started from Mr. Swinburne's
over-pitched praises.   I had said that I thought
the poem neither 'equal' in its 'elevation' throughout all parts of it, nor pure in its excellence;
and I had to make this good by reasons.   The
poem is not a perfectly fused whole; but perhaps
just in the struggle to be so it is more interesting than if the contention of its unclarified
elements were already allayed.   'Hardly a single
false note', 'purity of music', 'clarity of style'!
Even the *Ode to Evening*, beautiful as it is, is not
properly praised in these terms.

COLLINS: THE VOLUME OF 1746:

(*b*) THE PATRIOTIC ODES AND *THE PASSIONS*

I KNOW only one poem of Collins of which I should be prepared to say that it had 'hardly a single false note'; only one of which I should predicate 'clarity of style'; only one of which I should call the music throughout 'pure'. I mean the lines which begin 'How sleep the brave who sink to rest . . .'.

Of the patriotic Odes of Collins, this, as it should, leads the line in the volume of 1746. I am content, if we are to be obliged to range Collins' poems in an order of merit, to concede to Mr. Swinburne that the greatest of the Odes is that to Evening. But 'How sleep the brave . . .' is the most perfect. I do not know that there is anything that I would wish away from it. Its 'Pilgrim grey' and its 'weeping Hermit' trail, it may be, some cloud of 'Gothic' affectation. But the piece is at least near enough to perfect to make any critical objection ungracious. It is the only poem of Collins which moves with unarrested fluency,

with real inevitability in its sequences.   That is
the stranger from the fact that its perfections can
be shown to be hard-won.   For these two perfect
stanzas are, in truth, a kind of refashioning of
three stanzas of a far less perfect poem, the *Ode
on the Death of Colonel Ross.*   The later and greater
poem is well enough known for me to take it
here as read.   But I may be allowed to set out
the three stanzas from the earlier piece which
I speak of as a kind of first version :

> By rapid *Scheld's* descending Wave,
> His Country's Vows shall bless the Grave,
>   Where'er the Youth is laid :
> That sacred Spot the Village Hind
> With ev'ry sweetest Turf shall bind,
>   And Peace protect the Shade.

> Blest Youth, regardful of thy Doom,
> Aërial Hands shall build thy Tomb,
>   With shadowy Trophies crown'd :
> While *Honor* bath'd in Tears shall rove
> To sigh thy Name thro' ev'ry Grove,
>   And call his Heros round.

> The warlike Dead of ev'ry Age,
> Who fill the fair recording Page,
>   Shall leave their sainted Rest :
> And, half-reclining on his Spear,
> Each wond'ring Chief by turns appear,
>   To hail the blooming Guest.

How far more perfect the later piece is, how much superior in its concentration of power, I need not stop to urge. But it is worth remarking that the later piece, though more general in its reflection, carries more individual sentiment. The lines on Colonel Ross commemorate, we must suppose, a man whom Collins knew; in any case, they are a *consolatio* addressed to a person very dear to Collins, and to whom Ross had been very dear. Yet they want, for the most part, precisely that out of which it is reasonable to think they sprang—personal feeling. Ross' true memorial is 'How sleep the brave . . .'; in which, we may believe, the emotion aroused by the tragedy of his loss, after being stifled in its immediacy, later 'recollected in tranquillity' issues in that sublimed, and almost passionless, passion which (if poets may be believed) poetry is. Dr. Johnson, in his simple adequate fashion, has said of Collins that he 'did not sufficiently cultivate the sentiments'. It is one of those just remarks in which Dr. Johnson abounds, of which lesser critics are, from fear of the obvious, shy. Collins' poetry, as a whole, wants sentiment and mystery; and that is why no one, perhaps, has ever taken Collins to his heart; why he has commonly seemed more worthy of admiration than of love.

But 'How sleep the brave . . .' has that saving suffusion of sentiment which is wanting to most of Collins' pieces—even as the *Ode to Evening* bears just that gentle air of mystery, evening mystery, which belongs to some of the landscapes of, say, Ruysdael.   And thus it is a true instinct by which these two poems have commended themselves, above anything else of Collins, to the average student of poetry.

I have noticed already that the Ode on Colonel Ross is written in a metre in which Collins is never at his best.   The metre of 'How sleep the brave . . .' is the octosyllabic, with the couplets arranged in stanzas of six lines.   The pattern is used by Joseph Warton in his *Ode to the Nightingale*.   It is the merit of Collins' two stanzas that each of them, rhythmically, has the true seventeenth-century culmination.   The subtle means whereby the movement of the stanza culminates, rather than collapses, was the grand secret of the 'metaphysicals'.   Collins knows it, here and elsewhere (he uses his knowledge very effectively in the *Ode to Simplicity*) ; and the Wesleys also know it, in some of their best hymns.

In the same metre as the poem on Colonel Ross is written the *Ode to Peace*, misplaced in Collins' book, so that it follows on the *Ode to*

Evening. Perhaps it hardly deserved a place in the book at all. It opens badly:

> O Thou, who bad'st thy Turtles bear
> Swift from his Grasp thy golden Hair,
> And sought'st thy native Skies:
> When *War*, by Vultures drawn from far,
> To *Britain* bent his Iron Car,
> And bad his Storms arise!

'Clarity of style'! But it takes some pains to discover that 'his', in line 2, refers to *War*, who, despite the colon at the end of line 3, is not mentioned until the fourth line. (There is the same obscure use of the pronominal adjective in lines 9 and 23–4; and it is, as I have said already, a characteristic blemish of Collins' style.) In the fourth line, I have to think twice before I am sure that it is, not the Vultures, but *War* that is 'drawn from far'. Of the incongruous picture furnished by this first stanza—in which Peace bids her Turtles to loose her golden hair from the grasp of the Vulture-charioted *War*—I prefer to say nothing. 'The British Lion, Goddess sweet', who, in the third stanza, kisses the feet of Peace, is almost equally disconcerting—till you make the discovery that the Goddess is, not the Lion, but Peace herself. If the truth must be told, no single stanza of this Ode has any redeeming felicity of sentiment, thought, or phrase.

There remain, of the patriotic Odes, the *Ode to Mercy* and the *Ode to Liberty*. The former of these two pieces is believed to have had for its occasion the circumstances following upon Culloden; to be a plea for clemency towards the men who came out in 'the forty-five'.[1] If it be compared with the *Ode to Peace*, it seems likely that the two poems were written in somewhat close conjunction. *Mercy*, however, has merits which *Peace* lacks. Not high merits; but the first section of the strophe (i. e. lines 1–6—for Collins has omitted to mark the sections here) has melody; and the strophe as a whole is an introduction to something better than its antistrophe. Even so, this is not a considerable poem. It was no easy task, one may think, to write patriotic poetry under the régime of the Pelhams; and Collins, it might confidently be affirmed, would have been well advised not to try it, save that, in this kind, he has left us 'How sleep the brave . . .'—and the *Ode to Liberty*.

The *Ode to Liberty* I do not admire as much as some persons; and very likely I admire it less than I should. Yet here again, 'What potentialities!' I am moved to exclaim. They are the potentialities of a Coleridge, a Shelley—the com-

[1] The precise reference in the line 'Where *Justice* bars her Iron Tow'r' eludes me.

parison with Coleridge, the Coleridge of 1795–8,
is one that again and again obtrudes itself.
Where, in this period of Walpoles and Pelhams,
Collins learned to conceive of Liberty so much
in the spirit of the great romantics, I do not
know. At least the opening of the Ode was
written under stress of the same occasions as
those which are believed to have prompted the
Ode to Mercy. Only so, I think, can we explain the
reference to the 'feeling Hour', in lines 13–16 :

> O Goddess, in that feeling Hour,
> When most its Sounds would court thy Ears,
>   Let not my Shell's misguided Pow'r [1]
> E'er draw thy sad, thy mindful Tears.

Mr. Swinburne, I feel, has praised the first part
of the Ode too much, and has exaggerated the
degree to which it deteriorates as it goes on. The
Ode, he says, 'after an overture worthy of Milton's
or of Handel's *Agonistes*, a prelude that peals as
from beneath the triumphal hand of either of these
demigods of music, steadily subsides through
many noble but ever less and less noble verses'.
The 'overture', certainly, is finely sonorous :

> Who shall awake the *Spartan* Fife,
> And call in solemn Sounds to Life,
> The Youths, whose Locks divinely spreading,
>   Like vernal Hyacinths in sullen Hue,

---

[1] In the original text there is a comma after Pow'r

At once the Breath of Fear and Virtue shedding,
Applauding *Freedom* lov'd of old to view?
What new *Alcæus*, Fancy-blest,
Shall sing the Sword, in Myrtles drest,
   At *Wisdom's* Shrine a-while its Flame con-
      cealing,
(What Place so fit to seal a Deed renown'd?)   1c
   Till she her brightest Lightnings round re-
      vealing,
It leap'd in Glory forth, and dealt her prompted
   Wound!

There are obscurities here which I am not sure
that I know how to resolve. Why, in line 1,
'*Spartan* Fife'? Who are the Youths of lines
3–6? By the '*Spartan* Fife' I used to suppose
Collins, to mean quite generally, a warlike strain—
some such warlike strain as that of Tyrtaeus;[1] and
perhaps actually to have in mind the well-known
march-song of that poet:

> ἄγετ', ὦ Σπάρτας εὐάνδρω
> κῶροι πατέρων πολιατᾶν,
> λαιᾷ μὲν ἴτυν προβάλεσθε,
> δόρυ δ' εὐτόλμως ἄνσχεσθε,
> μὴ φειδόμενοι τᾶς ζωᾶς·
> οὐ γὰρ πάτριον τᾷ Σπάρτᾳ.

[1] Cf. Ben Jonson: *A Vision of the Muses of his Friend
Michael Drayton*, 66–9:

> How do his trumpets breathe! what loud alarms!
> Look how we read the Spartans were inflamed
> With bold Tyrtaeus' verse; when thou art named,
> So shall our English youth urge on . . .

'The Youths' would, then, be, not any Spartan
youths, but the Athenian pair, not named, but
celebrated, in lines 7–12, Harmodius and Aristogiton. But Collins' editors seem to understand the
verses differently. They suppose the Youths to be,
not Harmodius and Aristogiton, but the warlike
youths of Sparta generally; they suppose Collins
to go, first to Sparta, and then (line 7) to Athens, for
examples of the spirit of Liberty. This has the
advantage that certainly these two states were, to
the poets of this time, the patterns of free govern-
ment. As such they figure in the second book
of Thomson's poem *Liberty*; and, if that were
not so dull a poem, and if Collins had not been
so lazy a man, I might think he had read it. On
the other hand, if the Youths are Spartan youths,
then I should be inclined to think them, not as
the editors do, *any* Spartan youths, but those two
pre-eminent Youths of Sparta, Castor and Pollux.
This Spartan pair will then balance well the
Athenian pair. The 'simplex horror decorus'
of the hair of the Spartans is noticed, as editors
point out, by the poet Statius :[1] but, as they do not
point out, with incidental reference to the Dioscuri:

> talem *Ledaeo* gurgite pubem
> educat Eurotas.

[1] *Silvae*, ii. 6. 45–6.

In lines 9–12, what is '*Wisdom's* Shrine', wherein Liberty awhile concealed her sword? I do not know, and no one tells me. But I conjecture that *Wisdom* stands for that patron Goddess of Wisdom, Athena; and that the Shrine is the Temple, in Athens, of Athena Polias, with which historians associate the 'Deed renown'd' of Harmodius and Aristogiton.

In what follows the 'overture', the transition from Greece to Rome is ill managed; the more so as the period of Roman freedom is not signalized at all, but the poet, with a haste neither effective nor easily explicable, comes at once to the overthrow of Rome and the destruction of her liberty by the 'Northern Sons of Spoil'.

Rome falls; but does not wholly perish. 'Remnants of Her Strength' are still found up and down Italy.

> Yet ev'n, where'er the least appear'd,
> Th' admiring World thy Hand rever'd;
> Still 'midst the scatter'd States around,
> Some Remnants of Her Strength were found.

Here, as so often, I am perplexed where no one else is. In the second line 'thy Hand' is the hand of Liberty, in the fourth line 'Her Strength' is the strength of Rome. But in the first line,

> Yet ev'n, where'er the least appear'd,

what meaning has 'the least'? Is not 'the' a mere blunder for 'She' (i. e. Rome)?

The whole of what follows, down to the end of the 'Epode', is much inferior to everything that has preceded. The antistrophe, however, is, if not good, at least interesting. It conveys us from the classical world, and the Renaissance, to 'Gothic' scenes and sentiment. It ends, it is true, with a quatrain singularly ineffective, in which Collins celebrates the 'blest Divorce' of England from France: countries which, once parts of a single continent, the sea has now happily severed. Most of the section, describing that distant geological period in which no sea separated Gaul from Britain, is well developed; and the patriotic reflection to which it conducts might pass if it had been better done.

I may be allowed to call attention to a note of Collins, appended to this passage. He does not, he tells us, 'remember that any Poetical Use has been hitherto made' of the 'Tradition' of a once un-severed England and France. I suspect that he had a bad memory. Use had, in fact, been made of the tradition, long since, by Drayton, in the eighteenth Song of his *Polyolbion*: a poem which we might have expected Collins to have looked into; for both the poem and Selden's notes to it

must have interested the Wartons.   I should not
be surprised if Collins had in fact read some of
it.   As has been pointed out by previous com-
mentators, the phrase 'watchet Weeds', in *The
Manners*, seems to come from *Polyolbion* (5. 13).

The final section of the poem, the second
Epode, may be conceived to correct the 'Gothic'
antistrophe by the description which it offers of
the now vanished Temple of Liberty, of which,
however, 'the beauteous *Model* still remains',
a Platonic Idea laid up in the heavens.   The
significant part of this description I have already
quoted :

> Ev'n now before his favor'd Eyes,
> In *Gothic* Pride it seems to rise !
> Yet *Graecia*'s graceful Orders join,
> Majestic thro' the mix'd Design.

In the concluding lines, Liberty degenerates;
she becomes an eighteenth-century 'Fair'.   You
can never trust Collins over any long stretch of
writing :

> Our Youths, enamour'd of the Fair,
> Play with the Tangles of her Hair.

Horrible !   'Were it not better done' not to
meddle with Milton at all than so to use him ?

I come last to the poem which Collins, for
whatever reason, placed last in the volume of

1746? Did he, like Wordsworth, regard last place as the place of honour? Or was this piece written last? I am inclined to take the first alternative. The reference in the *Ode on the Poetical Character* to 'the dangerous Passions', who 'kept aloof' when the Poet was born from the union of God and Fancy, suggests to me that, when this scene was described, *The Passions* may have been already written; though certainly I would not press what is the merest suggestion. But there is a close connexion, as we have seen, between the *Ode on the Poetical Character* and that to Simplicity; and there seem to me to be indications that the latter was written concurrently with *The Passions*, or nearly so. In the seventh stanza of *Simplicity* the words

No more, in Vale or Bow'r,
The Passions own thy Pow'r

might even be taken for a cross-reference to *The Passions*. *The Passions*, again, is called 'An Ode for Music'. It might better have been called an Ode *on* Music. It handles the theme of Music in a manner notably similar to that in which the *Ode to Simplicity* handles the theme of poetry. What is the matter with music, in *The Passions*, is what is the matter with poetry, in the *Ode to Simplicity*; the loss of *nature*. The ideal music is to be sought where the ideal poetry is to be sought—in Greece; and for one and the same reason. Greece first illustrated the power, in both arts, of *nature*. The actions and effects of the Passions which the Ode called after them describes are designed to illustrate the power of nature, and in doing so to point the contrast with modern music. In the 'lov'd Athenian Bow'r' Music 'learn'd an all-commanding Pow'r'. But whither now is that power fled?

> Where is thy native simple Heart,
> Devote to Virtue, Fancy, Art?
> Arise as in that elder Time,
> Warm, Energic, Chaste, Sublime!
> Thy Wonders in that God-like Age,
> Fill thy recording *Sister's* Page . . .

—the 'recording *Sister*' is, of course, Poetry, the natural poetry which the *Ode to Simplicity* honours.

The Passions is, certainly, the boldest of Collins' Odes. Being in truth, as I say, an Ode *on* Music, it necessarily comes into comparison with Dryden's Ode. But Collins is not merely courageous enough to risk the comparison, he deliberately, in the close of his poem, challenges it, when he speaks of

Caecilia's mingled World of Sound:

and at least once (with 'flying fingers', in line 89)
his phraseology seems consciously to recall Dryden.
He may be allowed to have caught from Dryden
three qualities which he exhibits here in greater
measure than in any other of his compositions:
swiftness, and fire, and variety of sound-effect.
His temperament, if it had less of power than
Dryden's, had more of true poetical quality. He
was not capable of some of Dryden's trivialities—
Dryden, if truth be told, does not always remember the breadth and depth and height which
separate the imagined Hall of his Macedonian
King from a London music hall. I feel this
(though I hardly dare say so) even in the pleasant
jingle of 'Happy, happy, happy Pair!'. If Collins, again, is sometimes too much afraid of the
language of prose, Dryden is often too little afraid
of it. The familiar touch in

'Twas sad by Fits, by Starts 'twas wild

offends in Collins, but would pass, perhaps, without remark in Dryden. Collins' more usual fault
is the opposite. When the eyes of *Revenge* start
out of his head, Collins says so, not plainly, but
in a manner more alienating than the most homely
plainness:

While each strain'd Ball of Sight seem'd burst-
ing from his Head

—seeming to think (if I may once more quote Dr. Johnson) 'that not to write prose is certainly to write poetry'.

In one particular Collins is plainly inferior to Dryden. Dryden's Ode is better conceived; and he has thought his way through it better. It has a developing conception; it moves to a plan; with each stanza there is advance; and the poem ends where it must. The conception of Collins is ragged; he moves to no particular end which can be seen beforehand and felt when it comes; and the order of advance is straggling. The behaviour of the Passions is everywhere in Dryden's Ode what it nowhere is in Collins'—an ordered succession of psychological happenings. Dryden was helped, of course, by having a story to tell. The Passions who, in Collins' Ode, on no particular day, and to no defined purpose, sound the various instruments of the 'Heavenly Maid', Music, are not only not part of an ordered story, but act under conditions which ('for Madness rul'd the Hour') carry caprice to a point where it ceases, sometimes, to be interesting. They appear in the order—Fear, Anger, Despair, Hope, Revenge, Pity, Jealousy, Melancholy, Chearfulness, Joy : I omit those Passions that are, not performers, but merely sit and listen, or

listen and leap. Why Love should be among the
inactive Passions, equal to no greater exertion
than that of shaking 'thousand Odours from his
dewy Wings', it is hard to guess. Whether,
again, Chearfulness should have a place among
the Passions at all may well be thought doubtful.
Nor is it easy to discover any principle determining precedence among the different Passions, nor
upon what principle the male and female sex is
distributed to them. The first four take for their
instrument the Lyre. But it is, I think, not
wholly captious to say that only Fear and Hope
really do anything with it:

> First *Fear* his Hand, its Skill to try,
>   Amid the Chords bewilder'd laid,
> And back recoil'd he knew not why,
>   Ev'n at the Sound himself had made.

Admirable! But then comes Anger:

> Next *Anger* rush'd; his Eyes on fire
>   In Lightnings own'd his secret Stings:
> In one rude Clash he struck the Lyre,
>   And swept with hurried Hand the Strings [1]

—and back recoiled—or what? The action of
Fear issues in an effect, which is given; and an
expectation is created that the effect of Anger's

[1] I have repunctuated the stanza—Collins' punctuation is
unintelligible.

action also will be stated or hinted.   But to the
action neither of Anger nor of Despair is any
effect attached.   With Hope we fare better:

> A soft responsive Voice was heard at ev'ry
>   Close,
> And *Hope* enchanted smil'd, and wav'd Her
>   golden Hair.

Something does happen—though the last five
words have, I feel, some touch of absurdity.

Revenge, who follows, both blows a trumpet
and beats a 'doubling Drum'.   In the pauses
'dejected *Pity*'

> Her Soul-subduing Voice applied,

—but to what, we are not told; nor does Pity,
I think, who has to get her word in edgewise
where she can between trumpet and drum, altogether escape out of the ludicrous.   Jealousy,
who succeeds, has no instrument, or none that
her poet thought worth speaking of.   But Melancholy 'pours thro' the mellow Horn her pensive
Soul'; and save for 'mellow Horn' she is well
described.   The 'mellow Horn' is also used by
Chearfulness.   But why these two opposed charac-
ters should share the same instrument I do not
divine.   Joy, by contrast, employs both pipe and
viol.   At least, I suppose him to employ the viol:
but he is, in fact, only said to *see* it.   Both Chear-

fulness and Joy, again, are, in their acts and circumstances, well described; and, indeed, lines 57–94 of this ode are as good both in diction[1] and in the quality of their music as anything in Collins. It must be added that both the prologue and the epilogue to the ode are in Collins' best manner. That the poem was written with something of the *furor arduus* proper to odic composition—at least that it was written in a hurry—may be inferred from the fact that two lines, 45 and 85, end in words for which Collins has forgotten to find rhyme-correspondence. About line 85 there may, perhaps, be some doubt; for it is likely, I think, that a line has been lost in the printing (we have already met what seems to be an example of the same carelessness at line 9 of the *Ode to Fear*). I have pointed out that, in lines 83–4, Joy is only said to *see* the viol; he is nowhere said to *sound* it. But 85 has

They would have thought who heard the Strain

—the strain which (unless a line has been lost) is not further hinted than by 'saw the brisk awak'-ning Viol' in 83. For two other verses (29 and 44) Collins *nearly* forgot to find the rhymes—

[1] Though the personification of 'Brown *Exercise*', in line 78, is infelicitous. Dyce notes that *Exercise* is already a person in Parnell's *Health : An Eclogue.*

we have to wait nine lines in the one case, ten in
the other, before he hands in the tallies. That
the ear of most readers, probably, misses these
negligences is a tribute to the spirit and beauty
of the poem as a whole.

The form of this Ode is unique in Collins. It
is the only One of his Odes which can properly be
called 'Pindarique'; the only one, that is, of the
'irregular' Cowleyish pattern—though Collins,
when he wrote it, modelled his style, not on
Cowley, but, as I have said, on Dryden. Already
in 1706 Congreve had urged truly that the 'Pindarique' species was a rather monstrous birth.
'I do not know', he writes, 'that there is to this
day extant in our language one Ode contriv'd after
his (Pindar's) Model'. There he was wrong—
there was one, which it was odd he should not
know, Jonson's Ode on Cary and Morison. 'The
Character of these late Pindariques', Congreve
continues, 'is a Bundle of rambling incoherent
Thoughts, expressed in a like Parcel of irregular
Stanza's, which also consist of such another Com-
plication of disproportion'd, uncertain and per-
plex'd Verses and Rhymes.' I do not know what
immediate influence either Congreve's admonition
or his example had upon the makers of Odes. But
it is worth noticing that the Wartons and Akenside

avoid 'Pindariques', the irregular Cowleyish Ode,
altogether. Nearly all their Odes are of the Latin
pattern; though, even before West's *Pindar*, both
Joseph Warton and Akenside had written Odes
which are so far Pindaric that they exhibit a dis-
tribution into strophe, antistrophe, and epode, and
preserve the correct correspondences (in fact,
neither of them uses the actual terms strophe,
antistrophe, &c.). I think it possible that both of
them may have had sight of West's *Pindar* before
it was published. Their Pindaric Odes are, in
any case, very little like Pindar, and very like the
Latin-pattern Odes which they commonly favour;
they exhibit little variety or complexity.

I may be allowed to note here an error in connexion with Warton and with West's translation of
Pindar which would be less important if it did
not find a place in the *Dictionary of National Bio-
graphy*, and if it had not propagated itself into
the *Cambridge History of English Literature*. The
Dictionary states that Warton's first book of verse
was his *Ode on Reading West's Pindar*. It dates
this Ode 1744, saying that 'it included, with other
poems,' *The Enthusiast*. The *Ode on Reading
West's Pindar* in fact appeared, as we might expect, after West's *Pindar* had appeared. Both the
Pindar and the Ode belong to the year 1749.

Akenside's *Odes*—the first book, I think, in this century of ode-making to bear the name 'Odes' on its title-page—was published in 1745. It contains an *Ode on Lyric Poetry* in which, speaking of Pindar, Akenside has the line

Behold the man of Thebes appears.

Not a particularly striking line. But it was good enough for Warton to echo in the second line of his *Ode on West's Pindar*

The man of Thebes hath in thy vales *appeared.*

The echo is interesting, since it raises the question whether, when he wrote his earlier Odes, Warton was already familiar with the Odes of Akenside; whether, again, Collins was familiar with them.

The 'irregular' character of *The Passions* is mitigated by the circumstance that it begins with a prologue of sixteen continuous octo-syllabic lines (rhyming in couplets), and has a similar series of twenty-four lines for epilogue. The prologue is followed by four octosyllablic quatrains, of which the first three are alternate-rhyming, while the fourth rhymes together its second and third lines only, leaving the first and fourth lines to pick up their rhymes in the first paragraph of the series of sixty 'irregular' verses which follows, and which constitutes the Cowley-pattern core of the Ode.

I have suggested that, placing this Ode last in his book, Collins gave it what he conceived to be the place of honour. But at a later date he outgrew, it would seem, his liking for 'Pindariques'. The Ode [1] was set to music in 1750 by William Hayes, who was for five and twenty years Professor of Music in Oxford. Collins, in a letter to Hayes, mentions that he had composed an Ode on the music of the Grecian theatre, which 'is probably more correct' (than *The Passions*), 'since I have chosen the ancient tragedies for my models': instead, he must mean, of Pindar. What a Pindaric Ode was in fact like he had, I imagine, no more idea than Cowley. In the same letter to Hayes he speaks of himself as having 'another more perfect copy of the Ode' on the Passions. Of this nothing is known; but that Collins especially valued this Ode is likely. In *The Manners* he speaks of himself (if I have rightly understood lines 49–52) [2] as 'by the Passions nurs'd'; and there may be some allusion there to *The Passions*:

[1] With a new conclusion, written by Lord Lichfield, and with Collins' ll. 93–end excised: see H. O. White, *Review of English Studies* iii, 1927, pp. 19–20.

[2] See above, p. 47.

An Ode. The Manners is Collins' earliest piece.
But I would not be certain that parts of *The
Passions* may not be earlier. Wooll, in his *Biographical Memoirs*[1] of Joseph Warton, has preserved
a prose fragment of Warton dating from his
schooldays ; of which he properly says that ' it is
no improbable surmise that the sketch furnished
Collins with the idea of writing an Ode on the
Passions '. It is worth while, I think, to set out
here a part of Warton's composition—we may
well agree with Wooll when he says that it
exhibits a *vivida vis animi* remarkable for the
years from which it sprang. *Reason* summons to
her presence her rebellious children :

'The first who made her appearance was *Fear*,
with *Superstition*, a pale-faced trembling virgin,
who came from Gallia, and was ever present at
earthquakes, fires, sieges, storms, and shuddered
at everything she saw. Not so *Anger*, whose
harbinger was *Cruelty*, with dishevelled hair ; and
whose charioteer, *Revenge*, drove wheels reeking
with blood. He himself stood upright, bran-
dishing a sword, and bearing a shield on which
was engraven Achilles dragging the carcass of
Hector, with Priam and Andromache lamenting
on the walls ; round his girdle he tied the head
of an enemy just slaughtered, and his chariot was

[1] pp. 11 sqq. (1806).

drawn by tigers. Next came *Joy*, chanting a song, crowned with vine-leaves, waving a rod in his hand, at whose touch everything smiled; he was attended by *Mirth* and *Pleasure*, two nymphs more light than Napæans; he was the institutor of feasts and dances amongst shepherds, at a vintage, at marriages and triumphs. Then came *Sorrow*, with a dead babe in her arms: she was often seen in charnels and by graves, listening to knells, or walking in the dead of night, and lamenting aloud; nor was she absent from dungeons and galley slaves. After her *Courage*, a young man riding a lion, that chafed with indignation, yet was forced to submit—not a fiercer roars in Ægypt whilst the pyramids reecho to his voice: naked, like an Englishman, blowing an horn, he was seen to attend Regulus to Carthage, Henry the Fifth to Agincourt, Moluc, Charles of Sweden, Kouli Khan, &c. He led *Cowardice* chained, who shuddered violently whenever he heard the horn, and would fain run away—so the beasts run when they hear the rattle-snake. Next came *Æmulation*, with harp and sword: he followed a phantom of *Fame*, that he might snatch the crown she wore: he was accompanied by a beautiful Amazon, called *Hope*, who with one hand pointed to the heavens, and in the other held an optic which beautified and magnified every object to which it was directed. *Pity* led her old father *Despair*, who tore his grey locks, and could scarce move along for extreme misery; she nursed him with

her own milk, and supported his steps, whilst
bats and owls flew round his head. She frequents
fields of battle, protects the slain, and stanches their
wounds with her veil and hair.   Next came *Love*,
supported on each side by *Friendship* and *Truth*,
but not blind, as the poets feign.   Behind came
his enemies, *Jealousy* who nursed a vulture to feed
on his own heart. *Hatred* also, and *Doubt* shaking
a dart behind *Love*, who, on his turning round, immediately vanish'd.   *Honour*, twin'd round about
with a snake, like Laocoon.   Then *Ambition* in
a chariot of gold, and white horses, whose trap-
pings were adorned with jewels, led by *Esteem*
and *Flattery*. *Envy* viewed him passing, and
repined like a pard with a dart in his side.   *Contempt*, too, like a satyr, beheld, and pointed with
his finger ; but he too often reviled Heaven,
whence plagues, pestilences, war, and famines.'

But *The Passions* should be read in connexion
with yet another composition of Joseph Warton—
and that his best.   It should be read in connexion
with the concluding lines of Warton's *Ode to
Fancy*, the first poem in his volume of 1746,
as *The Passions* is the last in Collins'.

> O Queen of Numbers, once again
> Animate some chosen swain,
> Who fill'd with unexhausted fire
> May boldly strike the sounding lyre,
> Who with some new unequalled song
> May rise above the rhyming throng,

O'er all our listening passions reign,
O'erwhelm our souls with joy and pain,
With terror shake, and pity move,
Rouse with revenge, or melt with love.

Without actually identifying the 'chosen swain' of these lines with Collins—or even while allowing him to be Warton himself—it is yet permissible to conjecture that the lines were not written without some thought of Collins' great Ode.

After 'How sleep the brave . . .' and *Evening*, *The Passions* is certainly the greatest of Collins' Odes. The present times are perhaps less favourable than most for the proper appreciation of it; for we have lost the taste for allegoric description. Yet in almost any period, it will be felt to want a sufficient *human* quality. It suffers from the same defect as characterizes, I have said, nearly all Collins' poetry: defect of sentiment and mystery. That Collins' nature was deficient in these qualities, I do not say. Against the first of them I fancy that he somewhat carefully schooled himself. He conceived poetry to have suffered too long from a plethora of moral reflection. He wished to bring back *description*. That he was qualified to describe—and to see—the *Ode to Evening* attests. In that Ode, at least, he sees finely a piece of the English country-side—like Gray's *Elegy*, the poem is, above all, English.   But he either could not, or would not, see men and women.   There is no man nor woman nor child in any poem that he wrote.

Thomson, if stanzas lvii–ix of the first Canto of *The Castle of Indolence* do, in truth, commemorate Collins and not, as some have supposed, William Paterson, Thomson has remarked on the power that there was in Collins to 'teach the noblest morals of the heart'; on the power that he had to do this, and the perversity with which he buried his talent :

But these his talents were y-buried stark ;
Of the fine stores he nothing would impart,
Which or boon nature gave or nature-painting
        art.[1]

[1] 'boon Nature' is Collins' own phrase (*The Manners*, 71). But I think Thomson's comment on the talent-burying disposition of Collins perhaps extends to more than his reluctance to impart *moral* truth.   *All* Collins' 'great ideas' 'fled and left no trace behind' (lix, 9).

COLLINS: 1749
GENERAL CONSIDERATIONS

IN the summer of 1748 Thomson died. What degree of intimacy had subsisted between him and Collins we do not know. He is believed to have introduced Collins to the Prince of Wales; a compliment which Collins was likely to feel, and which he returned, in nobler kind, by introducing Thomson to the Wartons. Nearly a year after Thomson's death, namely, in June 1749, Collins published in folio his *Ode Occasion'd by the Death of Mr. Thomson*. '*Amavit nos quoque Daphnis*', says the title-page; and prepares us for a private and human grief. 'Mr. Collins', says Langhorne, 'had *skill to complain*. Of that mournful melody and those tender images which are the distinguishing excellences of such pieces as bewail separated friendship, or beauty, he was an almost unequalled master. . . . From his own great sensibility he felt what he wrote'. This is all as it should be; and I could wish it true. Something of 'mournful melody' Collins' lines have. But neither the thoughts nor the phrases of his poem are those

which one would expect for the expression of a
personal and near grief.

> In yonder grave a Druid lies,
>   Where slowly winds the stealing wave !
> The year's best sweets shall duteous rise
>   To deck it's Poet's sylvan grave !

I feel with Mrs. Barbauld—with whom I do not
often sympathize—that 'there is no propriety in
calling Thomson a Druid or a pilgrim '.[1] Of the
third line, I have already remarked how justly
Tennyson censures its 'bad hissing' quality. Of
the second line, I may notice, accordingly, that,
weak as it is, Tennyson remembered it when he
made a strong line of his own :

> Thy marble bright in dark appears,
>   *As slowly steals a silver flame*
>   Along the letters of thy name,
> And o'er the number of thy years.

The reminiscence is a trivial matter ; but reminiscence there *is*. For just as Collins passes from
his picture of the river to the thought of the
church on its banks, where Thomson lies buried,
so Tennyson passes from 'that broad water of the
west' to the 'dark church' where 'like a ghost',
Hallam's tablet 'glimmers to the dawn'.

[1] The 'pilgrim' appears in line 12.

Through the first three stanzas, Collins makes
no effort to shake off the 'Druid' and the 'pilgrim'. But his fourth stanza promises more
natural notes :

Remembrance oft shall haunt the shore
  When Thames in summer-wreaths is drest,
And oft suspend the dashing oar
  To bid his gentle spirit rest !

This was the stanza that Wordsworth specially
remembered, when he wrote his own lines on
Collins. Collins' poem is believed to have been
'written in an excursion to Richmond by water'
(Langhorne) ; and this stanza half persuades us
that a personal theme is going to be treated in
a personal manner. But a moment afterwards
we discover that 'Remembrance' is, not a human
feeling, but a goddess. Other eighteenth-century
goddesses immediately throng to her aid, or her
confusion—Ease and Health and Love and Pity.

And oft as Ease and Health retire
  To breezy lawn, or forest deep,
The friend shall view yon whitening spire,
  And 'mid the varying landschape weep.

'The friend'! Just as we might think that
Collins was going to say something from the
heart, say something of himself and Thomson,

he drifts into that frigidity. And worse waits,
to wit—

> tears, which Love and Pity shed,
> That mourn beneath the gliding sail !

Not Collins' tears, not a man's tears, nor a poet's.
But the tears of two goddesses, who have been
placed for the occasion in a real sailing-boat, on
a real 'excursion to Richmond by water'. And
again, when at length, in stanza viii, Collins has
the courage to speak of himself,

> Now waft me from the green hill's side,
> Whose cold turf hides *the buried friend.*

'The buried friend'! What a corpse, in truth,
Collins has made of him !

Even so, there is a characteristic pathos in this
piece: though not that which there should be.
What is pathetic is to see Collins, every now and
again, coming to *the human point*, and pulling himself up just short of it. He is always just going
to lapse, humanly and truly, into '*my* friend', and
even 'my boat'; when some demon of anti-senti-
mentality calls him too loudly and harshly back
to the old conventions. It is this struggle in
Collins himself between genuine and factitious
that infuses the poem with a tenderness not to be
missed even by ears whom its false notes have

offended.   It is perhaps a compliment to the piece
that it suggests the reflection ' If Wordsworth had
done it ! '   But I am afraid that Mrs. Barbauld
must have it, this time, all her own way.   ' There
is nothing ', she says, ' characteristic of the Author
he wished to commemorate . . . [even] the church
of Richmond is not white, nor a spire, nor can it
be seen from the river '.

I say all this, or take what others have said,
and yet, though there is nothing of it that I do
not feel to be true, I am left with a perplexed
sense that this is a better poem than I seem to
have allowed—I had almost said, a better poem
than it should be.   It is easy to point out the faults
of it ; and hard to define its obscure excellence.
Yet when you have said what is the matter
with it—that it ails here, and here—you have
to reckon with some fundamental *rightness* in
it.   Wordsworth knew what this was ; and he
was not easily deceived into thinking the bad
good (in the poetry of others) or the false true.
I must leave it at that—this poem has some
fundamental rightness of life which will always
plead for it against all the critics.

To October of this same year, 1749, it has
been, until recently, usual to assign Collins'
' Dirge in Cymbeline '.   The piece was, in fact,

composed at least five years earlier; being first
published in the 1744 edition of the *Epistle to
Hanmer*.[1] Impersonal in tone, slighter in character
than the lines on Thomson, this poem is, in its
artificial kind, beautiful and even affecting, with
a truer 'skill to complain' than that which the
lines on Thomson show. Dr. Johnson sufficiently
admired it to print it at the end of *Cymbeline*,
when he edited his great *Shakespeare*. Perhaps this
is to throw it into too lofty a context. But Collins
has 'rifled' to fine purpose here the sweets of Elizabethan pastoral; and this delicate flower of song
carries with it airs from that 'breathing Spring'
which we know in, say, Fletcher's *Gentle Shepherdess*.

Of uncertain date, but first published in the
Gentleman's Magazine of February 1788, is the
Song. The Sentiments Borrowed from Shakespeare,
'Young Damon of the Vale is dead'. I have specu-
lated on what Wordsworth might have done with
the lines on Thomson; and 'Young Damon' is
sufficiently praised when attention is called to a
certain Wordsworthian quality which it has. I
suspect that, in determining Wordsworth's liking
for Collins, his *favouritism* in respect of Collins,

[1] Collins' reference, in the heading, to 'Theobald's *Edition
of* SHAKESPEAR' suggests that the verses were written before the
appearance of Hanmer's *Shakespeare* (1743).

the Thomson elegy and the two Shakespearian
Songs had at least as much influence as the
greater Odes.

Yet another 'Song—the Sentiments borrowed
from Shakespeare' has recently been claimed for
Collins; and with enough of plausibility to make
it worth while to give the piece here. It was first
printed anonymously in *Dodsley's Museum* of 1746,
with the heading 'A song. *Imitated from the* Mid-
summer-Night's Dream of Shakespear':

Lo here, beneath this hallow'd Shade,
  Within a Cowslip's Blossom deep,
The lovely Queen of Elves is laid,
  May nought disturb her balmy Sleep!

Let not the Snake or baleful Toad
  Approach the silent Mansion near,
Or Newt profane the sweet abode,
  Or Owl repeat her Orgies here!

No Snail or Worm shall hither come
  With noxious Filth her Bow'r to stain;
Hence be the Beetle's sullen Hum,
  And Spider's disembowl'd Train.

The love-lorn Nightingale alone
  Shall thro' *Titania's* Arbor stray,
To sooth her Sleep with melting Moan,
  And lull her with his sweetest Lay.

In 1810 the piece was printed among the poems
of Thomas Warton by Chalmers, who, in a note

on page 76 of his introductory *Life* of Warton, speaks of it as 'authenticated by Dr. Warton's autograph in his copy of the museum *penes me*'. It was first claimed for Collins by Mr. Iolo A. Williams in the *London Mercury*, May 1923.[1] Mr. Williams calls attention to the manner in which some of its phrases are echoed in other poems of Collins. (He might have noticed that the passage of Shakespeare which the poem professes to imitate is that from which Collins has twice elsewhere borrowed the expression 'leathern wing'.[2]) But Mr. Williams has weakened his case by a queer confusion. When Chalmers speaks of 'Dr. Warton's autograph', he means, of course, Joseph Warton. Mr. Williams supposes him to mean Thomas Warton. But Thomas is always '*Mr.* Warton', for the sufficient reason that he never proceeded from his B.D. degree to the doctorate. Of course, Thomas Warton knew well enough whether he himself had written the poem—if he wrote it, it was 'his best piece of poetry'. But Joseph Warton, in attributing it to his brother, might easily be mistaken—he died in 1800, and

[1] See also the same writer's *Seven Eighteenth-Century Bibliographies*, pp. 103-4, 1924, and Lane Poole's *Collins*, Appendix ii, 1927.
[2] See above, p. 14.

his autograph note in Đodsley may, therefore, have been written more than half a century after the poem was first published. Mr. Williams is perplexed as to how Thomas Warton came to 'authenticate it [the poem] as his own'. The truth is that he never did so; and the fact that he never did so, and that the piece never found a place in any edition of his poems, is a very good reason for assigning it to some one else. If it is to be assigned to some one else, who so likely as Collins? The poem was first printed on August 16, 1746. On August 1 of that year Collins was in Flanders, and likely to be there some little while, since he was 'just setting out for ye army'.[1] This might well explain why Collins did not find a place for the poem (if it was his) in the volume of 1746 (which was published in December).

I come back to the year 1749. In the last months of 1749 Collins made acquaintance with 'Douglas' Home. When, towards the end of the year, Home returned to Scotland, Collins was moved to address him in a poem which was first printed when Collins had been dead twenty-nine years: the *Ode on the Popular Superstitions of the Highlands*

---

[1] *Letters to Gilbert White of Selborne from Rev. J. Mulse.* See H. O. White, 'The Letters of William Collins', *Review of English Studies*, iii. 9, Jan. 1927.

of Scotland. There are many who think this poem,
which never received its author's *ultima manus,*
and remains in several of its stanzas lacunous, to
mark the highest point which Collins' genius attained. Perhaps its unfinished state has enhanced,
rather than diminished, its impressiveness. Certainly, it has passages of a sweet and grave beauty,
and in one at least of its stanzas it reaches a felicity not unworthy of Keats. But I cannot think
that Sir Edmund Gosse has praised it well
when he speaks of its 'pure lyric elevation and
rapture'. Elevation it has, or the best parts of
it have. But wings, fire, and all that swiftness
and urgency which belong to *lyric rapture,* seem
to me wanting. Even the best parts of it I find
too much laboured. But if it is neither Collins'
best poem, nor (what it could not be) his most
perfect, yet it stands, I concede gladly, above all
the rest in the quality of *marvel.* I feel no disposition to collect the faults of it, whether these
reside in an imperfect fusion of the thought,
through all the parts, or in isolated crudities of
diction; and I shall not vex with commentary,
such as I have bestowed on the different sections
of most of the other poems, a poem which Collins
never published, but of which the unfinished
glories invite 'our wonder and astonishment'.

I will set out here the whole of the ninth stanza ; and upon it, and upon the Ode as a whole, I will permit myself only so much of comment as to observe that already that direction of poetry which we call the romantic movement has not merely begun, but has vindicated to itself 'unbounded range':

Unbounded is thy range; with varied style
    Thy muse may, like those feath'ry tribes which
      spring
From their rude rocks, extend her skirting wing
    Round the moist marge of each cold Hebrid isle,
To that hoar pile which still its ruin shows :
    In whose small vaults a pigmy-folk is found,
Whose bones the delver with his spade up-
    throws,
    And culls them, wond'ring, from the hallow'd
      ground !
Or thither where beneath the show'ry west
    The mighty kings of three fair realms are laid;
Once foes, perhaps, together now they rest.
    No slaves revere them, and no wars invade :
Yet frequent now, at midnight's solemn hour,
    The rifted mounds their yawning cells unfold,
And forth the monarchs stalk with sov'reign
    pow'r
    In pageant robes, and wreath'd with sheeny
      gold,
And on their twilight tombs aerial council hold.

        *   *   *   *   *

When I delivered to the British Academy the
lecture upon Collins round which the foregoing
pages have built themselves, I was chidden for
being academic and too cold. I was speaking
to an academy ; and I had thought that it might
be permitted to me to leave aside the journalism
that so easily besets us.   But I had not wished to
be cold—cold to Collins, for whose poetry I feel
an especial tenderness.   I feel this tenderness ;
yet the more I study poetry, the more, if I may
say so, do I respect it ; and the more, accordingly,
do I discover in myself a disinclination, not merely
to call bad good, but to call that great which is
only interesting.   The more I read Collins' poetry,
the more impressed am I, not with its greatness,
but with its interestingness.   If that seems poor
praise, it must be because we do not sufficiently
realize, on the one hand, how rare the escape is,
for poets and men alike, from the dull into the
interesting, and, on the other, how special a form
of greatness poetry is : so special that we need,
in speaking of it, all the circumspection of words
that we can win to.   And not merely circumspection of words, perhaps ; but we require to cultivate, deep down in us, circumspection of thought
and feeling.   We need not be afraid of that ; for
in connexion at least with the greatest poetry any

contagion of priggishness easily and at once drops from us.

Seeking this circumspectness, and being persuaded that the cause of poetry is more often harmed than helped by a gushing appreciation, I have refrained from any 'general characterization' of Collins. Where I have criticized, I have given chapter and verse; and if this method of criticism is (as I willingly concede) not the best, at least it is better than the worst, perhaps even than the ordinary.

Of such general characterizations of Collins as I know, I am still inclined to think that Johnson's, unjust as it must, upon the whole, be accounted, is perhaps the least safely to be neglected. Johnson, even where he is least just, is never silly; and if, of his penultimate paragraph upon Collins, he had omitted the last clause,[1] his *Life* would read less like a death-sentence. At once the worst and the worst-written essay upon Collins is certainly that of Mr. Swinburne. I wonder how many persons, led by that essay to the subject of it, have been left angry with Mr. Swinburne, disappointed with Collins? When criticism leaves me thus angry and disappointed, very often I do what I would wish to commend to others. I turn

[1] I have quoted this above, p. 40.

from the critics who do not know their business
to a critic who nearly always does, Hazlitt. Hazlitt knows his business—if he sometimes dis-
charges it in a slap-dash and prejudiced fashion,
that is not because he does not know better, but
because he does. In default, therefore, of such
a general characterization of Collins as I feel not
competent to devise, I will set out here the single
paragraph which is all that Hazlitt has given [1] to
a poet with whom, none the less, he had real sympathy. In doing so, I will premise that I do not
find in Collins the *pathos* of which Hazlitt speaks
(unless he has in mind that kind of pathos which
I have conceded to the lines on Thomson). I cannot subscribe, again, to his praise of the *Ode to
Fear*; and though I think highly, as will have
been seen, of the *Ode on the Poetical Character*,
I cannot think Hazlitt reasonable when he puts
it above all Collins' poems. Hazlitt has just been
speaking of Young :

'Collins', he goes on, 'is a writer of a very different stamp, who had perhaps less general power of
mind than Young ; but he had that true *vivida
vis*, that genuine inspiration, which alone can give
birth to the highest efforts of poetry. He leaves

---

[1] In the *Lectures on the English Poets* (chap. v). But see
the *Critical List of Authors*, Works, vol. v, p. 374.

stings in the minds of his readers, certain traces of thought and feelings which never wear out, because nature had left them in his own mind. He is the only one of the minor poets of whom, if he had lived, it cannot be said that he might not have done the greatest things. The germ is there. He is sometimes affected, unmeaning, and obscure; but he also catches rich glimpses of the bowers of Paradise, and has lofty aspirations after the highest seats of the Muses. With a great deal of tinsel and splendid patchwork, he has not been able to hide the solid sterling ore of genius. In his best works there is an Attic simplicity, a pathos, and fervour of imagination, which makes us the more lament that the efforts of his mind were at first depressed by neglect and pecuniary embarrassment, and at length buried in the gloom of an unconquerable and fatal malady. How many poets have gone through all the horrors of poverty and contempt, and ended their days in moping melancholy or moody madness !

We poets in our youth begin in gladness,
But thereof comes in the end despondency and
    madness.

Is this the fault of themselves, of nature in tempering them of too fine a clay, or of the world, that spurner of living, and patron of dead, merit ? Read the account of Collins—with hopes frustrated, with faculties blighted, at last, when it was too late for himself or others, receiving the

deceitful favours of relenting Fortune, which served
only to throw their sunshine on his decay, and to
light him to an early grave.[1]   He was found sitting with every spark of imagination extinguished,
and with only the faint traces of memory and
reason left—with only one book in his room, the
Bible ; " but that ", he said, " was the best ".   A
melancholy damp hung like an unwholesome mil-
dew upon his faculties—a canker had consumed
the flower of his life.   He produced works of
genius, and the public regarded them with scorn :
he aimed at excellence that should be his own,
and his friends treated his efforts as the wanderings
of fatuity.   The proofs of his capacity are, his
Ode on Evening, his *Ode on the Passions* (particularly the fine personification of Hope), his *Ode to
Fear,* the Dirge in *Cymbeline,* the *Lines on Thomson's
Grave,* and his *Eclogues,* parts of which are admirable.   But perhaps his *Ode on the Poetical
Character* is the best of all.   A rich distilled per-
fume emanates from it like the breath of genius ;
a golden cloud envelopes it ; a honeyed paste of
poetic diction encrusts it, like the candied coat of
the auricula.   His *Ode to Evening* shows equal
genius in the images and versification.   The
sounds steal slowly over the ear, like the gradual
coming on of evening itself. . . . I should conceive

[1] The success, in fact, of which Hazlitt speaks, neither
threw sunshine on Collins' decay nor lighted him to an early
grave.   Recognition did not come to him till he had been in
his grave many years.

that Collins had a much greater poetical genius
than Gray: he had more of that fine madness
which is inseparable from it, of its turbid efferves-
cence, of all that pushes it to the verge of agony
or rapture.'

Printed in England at the OXFORD UNIVERSITY PRESS
By John Johnson Printer to the University